NEW FRONTIERS
OF THE MIND

WEST DUKE BUILDING, WOMAN'S COLLEGE, DUKE UNI-
VERSITY. THE PARAPSYCHOLOGY LABORATORY IS A
TWELVE-ROOM SUITE ON THE UPPER FLOOR, FRONT.

NEW FRONTIERS
OF THE MIND

THE STORY OF THE DUKE EXPERIMENTS

By

J. B. RHINE

Author of

EXTRA-SENSORY PERCEPTION

ILLUSTRATED WITH PHOTOGRAPHS

GREENWOOD PRESS, PUBLISHERS
WESTPORT, CONNECTICUT

5 8 2 6 9 7 6 3

Library of Congress Cataloging in Publication Data

Rhine, Joseph Banks, 1895-
New frontiers of the mind.

Bibliography: p.
1. Extrasensory perception. I. Title.
BF1171.R48 1972   133.8   71-178080
ISBN 0-8371-6279-3

Reprinted with the permission of Joseph Banks Rhine

Reprinted in 1972 by Greenwood Press
A division of Congressional Information Service, Inc.
88 Post Road West, Westport, Connecticut 06881

Printed in the United States of America

10 9 8 7 6 5 4

CONTENTS

Chapter

LIST OF ILLUSTRATIONS

This book owes its final form to so many hands that I could not call it mine without acknowledging the debt I owe to those who have helped me make it. The text itself will, I hope, make clear what a great part my co-workers have played in the research it describes. In the early stages of the Duke experiments, when help was most needed, it came unsparingly and generously not alone from my wife, Dr. Louisa E. Rhine, but from my colleagues, Professor William McDougall, Dr. Helge Lundholm, and Dr. Karl E. Zener. Mr. C. E. Stuart, Dr. J. G. Pratt, and Professor and Mrs. George Zirkle, all of whom participated as assistants in the first years of work, contributed a great deal to it, and my obligation to them is acknowledged with gratitude.

There is a small group of silent partners who have contributed the funds which maintain the present staff of our laboratory. The value of this timely aid is very great, and it is acknowledged here with the most profound gratitude. Without exception these donors have preferred to remain anonymous.

In the actual preparation of the text of this book I am particularly obligated to my wife and to my secretary, Miss Miriam Wickesser. To numerous other friends I owe many valuable suggestions.

J. B. R.

Long Beach, Indiana
August 10, 1937

NEW FRONTIERS
OF THE MIND

CHAPTER I

A Fundamental Question Reopened

BEHIND SEVEN YEARS OF PATIENT WORK BY A number of people, work of which this book is the essential story, lies a question very simple to phrase but extremely hard to answer: As human beings, what are we? What is our place in nature?

Man's first attempts to make clear to himself his own position in the universe gave rise to the various primitive religions. Later, with the development of culture, came the many speculative philosophies, theories concocted by the reason out of the tissues of untested logic. Within times historically recent we have advanced to surer ways of finding out the truth, to those devices for answering questions known as the methods of science. In this more secure approach we rely upon neither the proofless revelation of the primitive priest nor the unverified speculation of the ancient philosopher.

Science has long been closing in on the great central question of the nature of man himself. Centuries of study have enabled it to penetrate the secrets of his internal anatomic structure and the intricate functions of blood, glands, and brain. Step by step as it grew, science has been encircling the problems of man's bodily nature, his evolutionary origin, his heredity and environment, and even the fundamental physics and chemistry of his make-up.

But in spite of the brilliant intellects which have been brought to bear on it during a hundred years of psychologic research, one question about our fundamental nature remains conspicuously unsolved. It is the greatest of all puzzles about the nature of man: What is the human mind? Where does it belong, if anywhere, in the scheme of our knowledge as a whole?

2

The mind is still a mystery. Among the men and women most qualified to speak of its fundamental character there is little general agreement. As long as this holds true, the rest of us are in the dark about what and where we are in the universe of reality. For it is by what we are mentally even more than by what we are bodily that we identify and regulate ourselves.

I am driven to believe that the most urgent problem of our disillusioned and floundering society is to find out more about what we are, in order to discover what we can do about the situation in which we exist today. In the conduct of our personal and our group affairs, our various outward and inward lives, we recognize more and more the need for a profounder kind of self-knowledge than any former age has had. Until we know more about ourselves we must recognize that we are moving forward blindly in a world whose patterns are constantly more complex and hazardous.

Yet if a century of investigation by hundreds of able minds has left the nature of the mind still so profoundly obscure, it is not easy to go on hoping that beating the same pathways of research even for another hundred years will bring us to the goal. This unhappy prospect compels us to look for some alternative, to seek out a new approach, perhaps one that in an earlier day it was easier to overlook. If the recognized and the usual in our search have so far failed us, it is time to turn, in the matter of our method, to the *un*recognized and the *un*usual. In the history of more than one branch of research a long-unrecognized phenomenon has turned out to be the key to a great discovery. The stone which a hasty science rejected has sometimes become the cornerstone of its later structure.

3

It has long been a common assumption among the learned that nothing enters the human mind except by way of the senses. The organs of sight and hearing, of taste and smell, and the other "receiving stations" in the skin and deeper tissues are the sole means by which we can perceive what is going on in the world outside ourselves. According to this long-unquestioned doctrine there is no way of di-

rect communication between one mind and another
and no possible means by which reality can be experienced except through the recognized channels
of sense.

So the mind is believed to be geared to the sense
organs, and they in turn to the mechanical world
about us. The energy of light makes vision possible,
mechanical vibration is the basis of hearing, and so
on. The human mind is ultimately dependent upon
the complex chain of mechanical principles. Hearing, for example, begins with a series of sound waves
which the various links of mechanical principle in
the ear transform to nerve impulses. The nerves
themselves, and the brain, are an elaborate mechanism, and so ultimately we hear. The more mechanical energy there happens to be in the instrument
from which the sound is produced, the more sound
we hear. It is a lawful and quantitative relation.

Starting, then, with the assumption that the recognized senses are the only ports of knowledge, the
conviction has grown upon most of us that mind,
too, is subject to the laws of the mechanical world.
For many people the infinitely complicated mechanics of the brain suffice to explain the deepest
secrets and mysteries of mental life. As a conse-
quence of this trend of thought, man himself has
come to be regarded as a vastly complicated machine—admittedly one that is conscious of itself
and about which many things are still mysterious.
Whether we like it or not, our first problem is to

settle the truth or error of this doctrine, and face the truth when it is ultimately established.

4

Apparently the only way the question can be decided is to find out whether or not the recognized senses are the only channels through which the mind can perceive. Suppose we assume for a moment that they are not. Suppose, to use another figure, the old frontiers of the mind that bound it by the limits of the recognized senses are not the true limits of the human personality in its universe. If we could prove this clearly and beyond dispute, if we could free the mind from the absolute restrictions of the mechanism of the senses, the effect upon the science of the mind—psychology—and upon man's whole view of himself would be almost too great to conjecture.

All of us are naturally on guard against ideas so revolutionary that they upset our thinking, and wisely so. But the urge to explore our inner nature, to know where we belong in the cosmic system about us, will not let us rest until we find out the truth, whatever it is. And that truth must be established, before we can accept it, upon actual experimentation, critically and deliberately conducted, which yields results that leave only one possible interpretation.

The experiments described in this narrative of

research in our laboratory at Duke University were undertaken with the express purpose of cornering the problem of whether anything enters the mind by a route other than the recognized senses. The answer which those experiments have yielded must be weighed carefully, and by each person in accordance with his own basis for judgment. It is an answer that is frankly presented as only a beginning on the great problem with which our work has been concerned.

The research described in the pages which follow is still going on actively and on a constantly wider front. Those who read this report of its first findings will, I hope, share something of the genuine excitement and joy of adventure which we who are engaged in the exploration are experiencing.

CHAPTER II

From Experiences to Experiments

THERE IS A COMMON BELIEF AMONG ALL PEOPLE that the reports of the recognized senses are not the only ones which the mind ever receives. Through all the ages of recorded history men have believed in the validity of intuitions, "hunches," mind reading, monitions or warnings of various sorts, and similar apparent manifestations of the mind's power to penetrate beyond the bounds of the mechanical and sensory world. Of course these beliefs have no place in the catalogues of scientific knowledge, and they are today quite widely supposed to be sheer superstition, error, or various forms of self-delusion.

Yet even if a traditional belief has no standing in science it may be used by an investigator as an indication of where to look for something new and possibly important. In his work of research the scientist begins with something which he cannot explain. It challenges him to find out about it, and science is mainly a way of finding out things.

2

When I was a boy in the mountains of Pennsylvania, belief in omens, warnings, or messages from unseen agencies was not uncommon among the people of the region. I remember hearing many stories of that unusual character which is loosely called "psychic" and which involved the acquiring of information without the use of the known senses. My father, however, was wholesomely skeptical of all such beliefs and tales; he taught me to dismiss them as superstitious nonsense. His attitude was one common to intelligent men in general, not only of his own time but of the present, particularly in various fields of science; and nothing in my early education encouraged me to any belief or even interest in such affairs.

Later, when I was a graduate student at a large university, one of my most respected science professors related a typical psychic occurrence to which he had been in part an eyewitness. The story, one of "seeing" beyond the range of the senses, of a vision apparently clairvoyant, is a good one of its kind, and I give it as it was vividly impressed on my memory twenty years ago:

"Our family was awakened late one night by a neighbor who wanted to borrow a horse and buggy to drive nine miles to a neighboring village. The man said, apologetically, that his wife had been wakened by a horrible dream about her brother

who lived in that village. It had so disturbed her
that she insisted he drive over at once to see if it
was true. He explained that she thought she had
seen this brother return home, take his team to the
barn, unharness the animals, and then go up into
the haymow and shoot himself with a pistol. She
saw him pull the trigger and roll over in the hay,
down a little incline into a corner. No reassurance
could persuade her that she had only had a nightmare. My father lent them a buggy (it was before
the day of telephones) and they drove to her
brother's house. There they found his wife still
awaiting her husband's return, unaware of any
disaster.

"They went to the barn and found the horses un-
harnessed. They climbed to the haymow, and there
was the body in the spot the sister had described
from her dream. The pistol was lying in the hay
where it would have fallen if it had been used as
she had indicated and if the body had afterward
rolled down the incline. It seemed as though she had
dreamed every detail with photographic exactness.
I was only a boy then, but it made an impression
on me I've never forgotten. I can't explain it and
I've never found anyone else who could," the professor concluded.

His story puzzled and impressed me when I
heard it, and it has remained in my mind long years
after most of the things he taught in class have
been forgotten. It is not the story alone that I have

remembered, but the fact that the man who told it, himself a teacher and a scientist, though clearly impressed by the occurrence, had no explanation whatever to offer; that he had lived all the years of his manhood believing such a thing had occurred and had done nothing, even to satisfy his own curiosity, about it.

At that time I had never before heard so clearcut and impressive a psychic story, certainly not from a person of such intellectual standing, a scientist with an international reputation. As a scientist he was an indefatigable worker. He would have been the first to utilize for study and investigation any new fact that came to his attention in his own department of knowledge or one allied to it. But this startling incident, which seemed to point so definitely to possible revolutionary facts in the interpretation of the working of the mind, he could allow to lie uninvestigated throughout his lifetime.

We graduate students did the same. We heard the story. We were impressed by the possibilities it suggested. We believed the facts, for we knew that the man who told it was as sane and balanced as anybody anywhere, and one whose scrupulous personal, as well as scientific, honesty was unquestioned. We did not accuse him even of unconscious exaggeration due to bad memory. We could not explain the story either—but still we did not do anything about it. I know now that the reason was that, after all, we did not fundamentally believe it. We did not know *how* we disbelieved it, since we did not doubt the professor's truthfulness. But one simply could not believe a story like that.

It can be said in extenuation that our group of graduate students were not psychologists. Such a story was not "in our line," nor were we competent to weigh and pass upon strange happenings in the realm of the mind. But if the story had been told to a group of psychologists, would their reaction have been different? Would they have pondered this strange occurrence, discerning in it a possible key to a revolutionary concept of the human mind? No, they would have disbelieved it too. They might have been somewhat more specific in their disbelief. Perhaps they would have said, "Ah, but he has no documentary evidence, no independent witnesses. He can't prove it." And so they, too, would have dismissed the story.

Suppose the professor had been able to hand over signed letters from the people concerned, suppose he had had real, objective proof that the facts of the occurrence were as he told them, would that have made any difference? Would his story even then have revolutionized science? Of course not. Somehow it would still have been questioned.

A more recent and better witnessed example of this same kind of thing is a story lately told in a public address by a well-known college president, a man whom no one who knew him would accuse of falsehood. He said that he dreamed very vividly one night of an old schoolmate. He had not heard from this man for many years. The dream, however, was so vivid that it stayed in his mind after he woke up. He told his family about it at breakfast and said he would like to write a letter to his old school-mate. A few days later he received a letter from the man, saying that he was writing after all these years because the night before (it proved to be the night of the college president's dream) the writer had had such a vivid dream of his old friend that he could not resist the impulse to send him a letter!

In this case there were independent witnesses in the other members of the family who heard the story of the dream at the breakfast table, and the letter itself was documentary dated evidence. Cases like this with even more and better documentary evidence are not lacking. To anyone making a study of such strange and inexplicable happenings it quickly becomes evident that both these stories are fairly common instances of a large group or class of inexplicable events. Both stories imply the ex-istence of strange, unrecognized powers of mind which we ought to know about if they are facts. But, however much we may be impressed, most of us are still skeptical. Scientists are almost sure to be so.

Since the college president's story has support-ing evidence, some other way to avoid believing it must be found. Perhaps these two old classmates received alumni bulletins from their school on the same day. Possibly this led their thoughts in the same direction and in the semiconsciousness of sleep caused each to dream of the other. Unlikely as this explanation may sound, it is a way to avoid believing anything so unsettling as that these two minds established contact in spite of distance and the limitations of the senses, stirred up old memories, and caused each to write the other the next day.

It would make small difference even if it were possible to prove that no such alumni bulletin existed, or any other factor common to both men which could have revived old memories and caused them to dream alike. The scientific world and perhaps a large part of the lay public would still be skeptical. The resources of skepticism are almost infinite. Consider, for instance, another kind of case, this one, too, drawn from many similar ones.

The story was told me by the wife of a college professor. One afternoon she was playing bridge at the home of a friend. Suddenly she had an impulse to interrupt the game, go to the telephone, and call up her maid to ask if her baby was all right. She felt that she should not even finish the hand she was playing, but could think of no excuse to justify an interruption to her fellow players. With a severe struggle she was able to keep herself under control until the hand was finished. Then she excused herself hurriedly, rushed to the telephone, called her maid, and asked anxiously about the baby. The maid replied that the child was all right. Comforted, she returned to the game. When she got back to her house a short time later she found a number of neighbors there. The maid, very apologetic, met her at the door, uneasily explaining that there was nothing wrong with the child but that, a moment before the telephone call came, she had fallen from her carriage, been caught by her heels, and was hanging head downward. How long she had hung there no one knew exactly, but a policeman had happened by and rescued her. The neighbors, attracted by the accident, had advised the maid to say nothing over the telephone that would disturb the mother, since the child was actually all right by that time.

The facts in this case are unquestionable. The person to whom it happened told me the story at first hand. She gave me the names of several people who could verify the events at both ends of the telephone conversation. In this case, too, there does not seem to have been any preceding event that could have led up to the occurrence and caused it to happen at just that particular moment. The principle of the common reminder which we conceived as possible in the case of the college president and his friend could have no application here. Nevertheless, there is a way around believing that the predicament of the child could have reached the mother, who was far beyond range of sight and hearing. Perhaps it may not be regarded as a plausible one, but it must be recognized: coincidence. Even though the mother was not in the habit of calling up her maid when she was away from home, and had never done so before on this kind of impulse, even though she assures me that ordinarily she had ample confidence in her maid, there is still the possibility that the whole thing could have been an accidental coincidence, however unlikely that may seem.

3

"Chance coincidence" is a convenient answer to most reports of mysterious, puzzling, and apparently inexplicable occurrences. The letters that cross in the mail? Chance! The friend who calls on the telephone while one is looking up his number? Again, chance! The people one unexpectedly meets in strange places after thinking of them? A coincidence!

"Just chance" is a convenient explanation, and one that usually cannot be controverted, though it is a very unsatisfactory one. For layman as well as scientist it is always easier, and safer too, to be skeptical and conservative and to wait for proof before believing any fact which threatens to upset established beliefs.

However, remarkable stories are reported of inexplicable occurrences which even the "just chance" hypothesis has extreme difficulty in covering. One of my colleagues told me a story which was partly verified by correspondence, and which probably could be verified completely if it were essential. This story again is a type so common that almost everyone has heard a similar one.

A banker in a western state whose father was living in Alsace went to his office one morning and told the assembled board of directors the following story: The evening before, at about eight o'clock, he had picked up Willa Cather's *Death Comes to the Archbishop*. He had read the novel before, but now he turned, for no specific reason, to the description of the death of the archbishop and reread it. As he read, tears came to his eyes, and he was overcome by uncontrollable weeping. This seemed strange as he had not been so moved when he read the book the first time. He then remembered that the only other time he had wept since childhood had been at the death of his mother. He thought it might mean that his father had died, though he had no reason to imagine that there was any special danger of that's happening. Nevertheless, he made a notation of the exact time this conviction came over him. It was 8:10.

After relating the experience to his board of directors he wrote to his son, in another city, telling him about it and giving his own interpretation. When, later, he was notified of the death of his father and learned the exact time he found that, with proper correction for longitudinal differences, the day was the same and the time within a quarter hour of his notation of the experience.

In this case the evidence for spontaneous knowledge of an event happening thousands of miles away in Alsace is excellent. It is extremely difficult to doubt all the persons and papers involved. It is hard to suppose that there was some unconsciously used source of information, a recognition that at a certain season of the year a fatal illness might be likely to occur, or that the celebration of a particular occasion—an anniversary or birthday—might have proved too much for the father. In this, as in so many other cases that could be cited, it seems almost, if not entirely, impossible to find any reasonable way to avoid facing the idea that somehow the mind does sometimes traverse space and grasp things which the senses cannot perceive. The only escape is to cling to the hypothesis of coincidence.

Why is it that such a story does not revolutionize people's thinking about the human mind and its place in the world of space? Why are not psychologists eagerly snatching up the best of these stories and trying to fit them into a pattern to see what they mean? Entomologists with a new bug or beetle, geologists with a strange outcrop of rock, archaeologists with a newly located ruin to excavate, are eager to study and organize and classify. Yet the psychologists as a group ignore these strange occurrences in the realm of the mind. Only a few of them will even listen to stories of this kind, and the nonscientific world in general considers it more sensible to pay as little attention as possible. However impressive the evidence offered, it is easier, in general, to dismiss such a case, as my old professor did, simply by saying, "I can't explain it."

4

When many well-authenticated reports of such unusual occurrences are compiled (as they have been frequently, both here and in Europe), when these anecdotes have been sorted into types, classified and corroborated, the impression they make upon even the critical reader is considerable. On the other hand, few persons possessed of normal skepticism are compelled to a deep and moving belief in them. They are not of necessity led to suppose some extra-sensory way of knowing. They can still dismiss the whole business by saying, "I can't explain it."

This is because it is difficult to take these spontaneous happenings with full seriousness. If they are firsthand experiences, they may be harder to dismiss than if they are merely reported by somebody else; even so they usually *are* dismissed without any explanation. There is no way of coming to grips with them. They happen and are gone, leaving nothing but memory, none of the hard reality of a meteorite or a fossil.

What is needed to give them that sort of hard reality? The answer of science is this: When a group of facts or of alleged facts can be checked, reproduced at the will of an experimenter, varied and measured and tested, they take on an enormously increased reality. In this day of experimental science nothing so penetrates the skepticism that safeguards one's belief as the ability to produce at will, and to vary at will, the phenomena about whose objective reality there is doubt.

For this reason, then, if a scientific investigator —a psychologist or anyone else—wants to find out whether the human mind can upon occasion know things in a psychic or extra-sensory manner, he must turn from spontaneous cases of psychic occurrences, regardless of how interesting and dramatic they are, to definite, systematic experimentation. He must try to discover by repeated test, by careful laboratory techniques, whether there is anything behind the circumstances related in these stories. In short, the material within this field must be taken from the anecdotal stage to that of experimentation before it can be classified as scientific knowledge.

Yet, in passing from the anecdotal stage of this study to the experimental it is only fair to recognize what we owe to the anecdotes themselves. They have awakened interest in many minds, made an impression, raised the question as to whether or not there is some meaning behind them. They have made it evident that there is a problem for investigation. Certainly there could be no conceivable harm in making an investigation of these stories and their significance or lack of it. Any experimental investigation is bound to be a profitable one, even if it yields negative results. If it revealed, in this case, an important principle of nature manifesting itself in psychic occurrences and not yet catalogued by scientific knowledge, the search would surely have been worth while. And if the investigation proved that these episodes represent standard types of self-delusion inherent in the make-up of a great many people, that fact alone would constitute a real addition to knowledge as well as a salutary disillusionment.

CHAPTER III

Half a Century of Research

THIS BELIEF IN THE VALUE OF THE INVESTIGATION, regardless of whether the findings were positive or negative, was in all our minds when we began our research at Duke in the year 1930. We recognized that if psychic stories had any basis in fact there must be in the human mind a power or powers which could learn things without employing the ordinary sensory avenues of information. We began to call this ability to perceive things without using the senses "extra-sensory perception." It is a term that will occur often in this book.

We were far from being the first investigators to attack the problem of whether or not extra-sensory perception is a fact. An enormous amount of work was available for preliminary inspection, work that was of value in suggesting points of attack and methods of operation and, in a negative way, in warning us of the pitfalls into which some of the researches prior to our own had fallen. To understand the nature of our own approach to the problem of the existence of extra-sensory perception the reader must necessarily have some knowledge of what had gone before.

2

Anecdotes of psychic experience had failed to make an impression on the world of intelligent science, but so, too, had the results of fifty years or more of actual experimentation. The anecdotes themselves had led to collection and classification of psychic instances, and these collections in turn had suggested a number of theories. Theories had naturally led to experimentation, and actual research work on unusual powers of the mind had been going on for half a century and in a number of countries. Theories of telepathic thought transference, "mind reading," were most often found among the English investigators. The hypothesis of a sixth, or unknown or hidden, sense was popular among the French, from whom comes the word "clairvoyance"—"perceiving beyond the limits of the known senses."

The word "clairvoyance" has come to have so many unscientific associations that it may at first offend some readers to find it in this book. But it is used here purely in the sense in which I have defined it. Nothing is implied by it beyond evidence of knowledge which under the conditions could not have been gained through the recognized senses. Frederic Myers, who constructed the word "telepathy," suggested at the same time the word "telesthesia" as a companion term to be used in the sense in which we speak here of clairvoyance. For the general reader, however, it has the disadvantages of unfamiliarity and a highly technical sound, so it seems wisest to rely upon a careful definition of the basic, original meaning of clairvoyance.

But with all the half century of "psychic research," as the subject was called in England, there was little advance in the conquest of the scientific world, whatever real merits the work may have had. It is doubtful indeed if there were as many believers in telepathy or clairvoyance in 1930 as there had been in 1880. Also, it seemed doubtful whether, at the rate and in the way such research was proceeding, scientific recognition would ever come.

The past fifty years, as we have now recognized quite generally, was a highly mechanistic period, especially inhospitable to claims that did not easily fit into its intellectual pattern. Psychological journals have not been ready to print articles on telepathy and clairvoyance, and the evidence for them has been presented through easily ignored channels. But perhaps the most telling reason for the failure of the evidence to secure public confidence is that it has shown merely that these phenomena do occur, and almost nothing more. None of the work had gone far enough to show what might be the nature of such unorthodox phenomena, to find their relations or laws, or even the conditions under which they may be demonstrated. Even so, on a less revolutionary topic the proof would long ago have been strong enough; but with this subject, where doubt is intense to begin with, proof plus plausibility is necessary. To make plausible a new and strange type of phenomenon, it must be connected with the already known; in other words, it must be "naturalized."

The earliest attempts at experimentation were fragmentary, and there is ground for skepticism in connection with them. The first were bound up with the history of mesmerism. During the last quarter of the eighteenth century a German physician named Mesmer, then practicing in Vienna, made the tremendously important discovery that one person can influence another mentally in a curious and at that time wholly unknown way. This type of influence Mesmer named "animal magnetism"; those after him called it "mesmerism," and it has become well known to us today as "hypnotism." In recent years it has advanced to a respectable place among recognized psychological realities. Dr. Mesmer himself reported at least one instance of apparent extra-sensory perception. This was in itself a trivial incident; one of his patients in a trance was able to locate a lost dog. She "saw" it in her mesmerized state.

Among some of Mesmer's followers it became a common practice to rely upon this supposed ability for the diagnosis of and prescription for disease and the location of lost objects. The mesmerized subject believed he saw the invisible organ or distant and concealed object although the senses themselves could not have been of help. But the very precautions needed for this line of investigation are conspicuously absent from the reports available, and this makes any conclusion hazardous.

After the mesmerists, some of the hypnotists took over the earlier view that the mind could go out through space and bring back knowledge of events which the senses could not possibly reveal or the reason infer. They even left reports of hypnotization at a distance, which would have required telepathy after the manner of Svengali in the story *Trilby*.

The fact is that some of the early experiments with psychic phenomena were carried out by medical men in good standing or by scientific men from the universities, but that was not by any means enough to make the subject acceptable to the general body of scientific men. When Professor (later Sir) William Barrett, a physicist from the Royal College at Dublin, read a report of his experiments on hypnotization and extra-sensory transfer of thought before the British Association for the Advancement of Science in 1876, his paper was received with open ridicule and was refused publication in the *Proceedings* of the Association. This refusal was not on the ground that vital flaws were found in his experiments, but rather because to scientists of that day such things as he reported were totally incredible.

In the eighties and nineties many university men became interested in the problem of extra-sensory perception, but at that time there was no university that would admit the problem within its walls as a project for academic research. Much of the genuinely novel exploration that calls for going beyond existing lines of respected knowledge in any department has had to be done entirely outside of university halls or quietly in some inconspicuous corner of the academic attic.

There is a good deal to be said in defense of the universities on this point. It is essential that they maintain respect and prestige, and to do so they must be conservative. Because of this unreceptive attitude on the part of universities a group of scholars who wished to work on telepathy and kindred subjects in the eighties formed—in England and later in America—societies to foster research in this field. The English Society for Psychical Research was founded in 1882 with the declared intention of investigating thought transference, telesthesia, hypnotism, the phenomena of spiritualism, and allied fields. Through the succeeding years the Society has followed its ideals of scholarly investigation of these subjects and in spite of many handicaps has contributed some careful experimental studies on the problem of extra-sensory perception and related lines. But, while it has won recognition and support from many individual scientists, particularly in England, it has not carried the day with the scientific world, which in the main has paid small attention to the Society and its publications.

What the Society has done is to carry the torch of experimentation from the storytelling, pre-Society period up to the present day, when it begins to look as though the universities will accept it and carry it on.

3

The earliest report made by members of the English Society for Psychical Research was a study of the Creery sisters. There were five of these girls, daughters of a clergyman in England. They showed such striking capacity to guess words, numbers, objects at which another person was looking that the father wrote to the new Society and asked to have an investigator come and study their case. Professor Barrett and a number of other prominent British men of learning took part in the investigation that followed.

The investigators selected a playing card, number, or similar object while the girl being tested was out of the room. Then they called her in and asked her to name the thing they had in mind. At first the proportion of successes was astonishingly high. Tests were carried out on various occasions over a period of a year or more. On the later occasions the successes, though still more than one would expect from chance, fell off considerably from their original number. (The reader may wonder how scores in this type of test may be considered high or low in relation to chance or luck. The evaluation is a relatively easy one and will be presented in full later in this book.)

Toward the end of the investigation, during a period of comparatively unsuccessful work, the investigators detected the girls in the act of trying to signal each other. It is typical of the necessity for extreme caution in investigating extra-sensory phenomena that the mere fact of the girls' communicating with each other was enough to discredit the investigation as scientific evidence. No one has been able to discover grounds for discarding the better part of the work, since the girls did not know what object they were supposed to perceive telepathically. Then, too, it is a poor kind of cheating which grows worse with practice, and the sisters had been most successful at the beginning of the investigation. Yet the mere presence of trickery—even such pointless and ineffective trickery as the Creery sisters apparently attempted—casts a doubt over every aspect of the case.

Professor Charles Richet, a distinguished physiologist of the Faculté de Médecine at the University of Paris, experimented with a hypnotic subject called Leonie. He found that she could call correctly an amazingly large number of playing cards sealed in opaque envelopes; that is, she could do so in Paris. When brought to England to demonstrate before a group of Englishmen she was unable to produce significant work. That was sufficient to satisfy some persons that there had been a flaw in her achievements in Paris. But we must in fairness grant that something like stage fright may have affected Leonie. Perhaps a French composer could not have written an acceptable sonata under such conditions in England either, with a committee scrutinizing every move. But no quarter can be granted to a claim so difficult to prove as that made for Leonie by Professor Richet. The critical public has felt little confidence in the ability of experimenters to deal with the possibilities of trickery. Obviously the most highly watchful attitude is justified on a point so important as this.

In addition to the Creery case there is another early study of telepathy that illustrates this necessity, the work done with G. A. Smith by the experimenters of the English Society for Psychical Research. Smith was a hypnotist, and he hypnotized subjects for work in tests for thought transference. In some of these cases the hypnotized person and the experimenter, or person supposed to be "sending" the telepathic impulse, were in separate rooms. Blocks from the old game of lotto were used to supply the numbers to be guessed, so that the value of the results was easily calculated. It was a great blow to the research when Smith later claimed that he had deceived the experimenters. It is hard to see how he could have, if the conditions were as reported.

Trickery need not be conscious in order to be effective, or voluntary in order to be a danger to an experiment. When Professor A. Lehmann, a Danish psychologist, raised the question as to whether "involuntary whispering" could explain the English Society's results in thought transference he showed that involuntary whispering did occur with some people when they were thinking intently and that under certain circumstances which he devised in his laboratory others could be guided by it.

Professor Lehmann, however, was a thoroughly open-minded critic, and when Professors Henry Sidgwick, of Cambridge, and William James, of Harvard, pointed out that this criticism could not have been a valid one in the experiments concerned, especially in those in which there was a closed door between the subject and the sender of the thought, he recognized that his theory could not hold and that thought transference must be the explanation of the results.

But Professor Lehmann's conversion is relatively exceptional, and the great body of experimentation conducted by research societies in France, Germany, England, and America did not succeed in gaining a substantial foothold in the scientific world.

4

The first attempt by a university to grapple with this problem only gave the subject a further set-back. About twenty-five years ago Stanford University received a large endowment for the promotion of psychic research, and Professor John E. Coover was put in charge. In 1917 he published a 600-page volume reporting the conclusion that, in the subjects he tested, thought transference was not present. The size and detail of the report gave it the appearance of being exhaustive, and the fact that it was done in a university of good standing and in a department of psychology had the effect of delivering a crushing blow to the remnant of interest still existing among scientific men. Coover's work became the classic investigation of psychic phenomena for those university circles in contact with the subject of psychic research. It was regarded as an authoritative scientific treatment of the subject.

Professor Coover's expertness was apparently demonstrated by an elaborate statistical evaluation of his results, and there seemed no further point in investigating extra-sensory perception. There the matter rested for a number of years. Then various other persons—five to my present knowledge—independently re-evaluated by standard procedures the results of Professor Coover's experiments in thought transference. They are unanimous in the conclusion that he is mistaken, that his results are not, as he thought, explainable by chance alone, and that he did in fact unwittingly have evidence in favor of thought transference.

Another pioneer among the American psychologists who have made investigations in this sphere was the late Dr. Edward B. Titchener, well-known psychologist of Cornell University. He wrote a paper in which he reported some tests conducted to find out whether people could tell reliably when they were being stared at from behind. He concluded that they could not, and also reached some negative conclusions on the possibility of conveying images telepathically.

According to one of Dr. Titchener's Ph.D. graduates, he was afraid to trust the laws of chance. He was not familiar with the methods for statistical evaluation. "On one occasion," this graduate reports, "a subject called almost entirely correctly down through a pack of playing cards, naming both suit and rank. Professor Titchener was disappointed that the subject did not get every one correct. Only a perfect score would have convinced him of the reality of thought transference."

5

It may have been, then, through inapplication and misapplication of statistical method that these two investigations were fruitless for the advancement of the subject in university circles. The next case in the history of university explorations into perception without the recognized senses fortunately did not suffer the same fate.

In 1920 that explorer of many fields, Professor William McDougall, came to America. At Harvard he discovered, lying in idleness, a fund for the support of psychic research and he put it to work, with Dr. Gardner Murphy and, later, Dr. G. H. Estabrooks as investigators. Although Murphy's work did not lead him to conclusive, publishable results, it made him an inveterate investigator of these problems. Estabrooks, however, in an experimental series that is beyond serious criticism, got results that seemed clearly indicative of telepathy. He used a large number of subjects, each of whom guessed playing cards for about half an hour. He placed subject and sender in separate rooms. The ready signal was given by a telegraph key which clicked every twenty seconds during the experiment. The subject wrote down the name of the first card that occurred to him after the click. The sender, at the same instant, was concentrating on a card chosen by a random cut from a shuffled pack before him.

At the end of a large series of trials the results, while not extremely far above chance, were high enough to prove statistically that something more than random factors was affecting them. The conditions adequately excluded any kind of sensory knowledge. The conclusion that there had been a certain amount of thought transference seems inescapable. Few scientific people know of this work, although it was done at Harvard University under the supervision of a world-famous psychologist. When considered seriously it is one of the most revolutionary accomplishments in the history of psychology, if not in the history of science; and yet no report of it appeared in a single psychological journal.

There is a still more precise experimental performance reported by Professors Henri Brugmans and Gerardus Heymans at the University of Groningen. In their psychological laboratory they found a young man who seemed to show an unusual capacity for thought transference. Estabrooks had worked with anyone he could induce to come into his laboratory, but Brugmans first selected from a larger group the most promising subject and then concentrated his experiments upon him alone. Also, instead of placing sender and receiver in two rooms on the same floor, Brugmans stationed them in rooms one above the other with a hole in the ceiling between them covered by two layers of plate glass, with an air chamber between to prevent possible sound cues. Through this plate-glass aperture the sender looked down on the hands of the receiver, who was seated at a table below. The latter was blindfolded and a heavy curtain screened his eyes from the table and the ceiling. On the table lay a checkerboard with forty-eight squares. While the receiver held a pointer in his hand, which was thrust through the screening curtain, the sender attempted to "will" the receiver to move the pointer to a specified square. Where chance or luck would have resulted in about 4 accurate indications of the square mentally selected by the sender in 180 trials, the actual scores ran up to the extraordinary total of 60.

It is difficult to find anything wrong with the technical details of this work. But it, too, was not published in a psychological journal, nor was it seriously regarded by psychologists. Like Estabrooks's work, it appeared only in the journals of psychic research organizations.

Another remarkable study which failed to gain recognition from psychologists in spite of its being one of the best and most unusual that have ever been reported was one made by the author, Upton Sinclair. Although professional scientists largely disregarded it, Sinclair described the experiments in a book entitled *Mental Radio*. The basic phenomenon which he had to report was the transfer, probably by telepathy, of images of drawings. One person, usually Sinclair himself, concentrated upon the particular drawing, while the receiver, Mrs. Sinclair, attempted to reproduce the image in the sender's mind. The comparisons between the original drawings and the images reproduced by the receiver are amazing in their correlation, but the experiment was not carried out under laboratory conditions. In fairness to Sinclair's work, however, it must be admitted that in this case such a distinction was a comparatively superficial one.

6

Although a highly critical group of scientists may possibly be forgiven for discriminating against an extra-academic study like Sinclair's, it is harder to understand how the work of Estabrooks and Brugmans could be passed over as casually as it was. Neither then nor now could anything fundamentally damaging to the good faith and scientific regularity of their work be said. It was not answered effectively by any member of the scientific fraternity. The reason for that may be that people, no matter how logical and scientific they aspire to be, do not have enough confidence in scientific method to trust a fact established by it *unless they can in some measure understand that fact* and fit it into the general pattern of their other beliefs. As a rule, a new and unexplained phenomenon is hard to believe in proportion as it is hard to understand.

The trouble with the early researches was that even if they established the *fact* of perception beyond the senses, they did not succeed in relating it appreciably to the rest of scientific knowledge. And so, it seems to me, the early work was largely lost so far as the world of science was concerned because it did not go far enough into the nature of the phenomenon reported.

This is necessarily the barest outline of the experiments which had been conducted prior to the start of the Duke research. In the sum total they were impressive, but as a whole they had failed to convince scientists or the world in general. Beyond the task of establishing the fact of perception without the use of any recognized sense, it remained for any future research to answer the questions: "What is the nature of extra-sensory perception? How does it work? Where does it fit into the scheme of things?"

CHAPTER IV

The Start of the Duke Experiments

IN 1930, NO AMERICAN UNIVERSITY WAS INVESTI-gating extra-sensory perception. When the four members of the Duke psychology department determined to study telepathy and clairvoyance as one of their laboratory research problems, it was the first time in the history of the subject that such a concerted attack had been made upon it by a group of university staff members, and the first time that a college department of psychology had given so much attention to the problem.

In any well-established branch of research a discussion of the actual personnel which conducts it is not necessary, for science is supposed to be largely impersonal. But in a pioneer project such as the one upon which the four of us embarked, the personalities of the men concerned are of obvious importance, if only to explain why they undertook to examine a field in which no other psychology department appeared to be working. For that reason I shall say a few words about these men, Professor William McDougall, Dr. Helge Lundholm, and Dr. Karl E. Zener, and about the circumstances of the origin of our co-operative research.

2

Professor William McDougall, F.R.S., the head of the department, is a veteran of many fields, among them that of psychic research. From his university days in Cambridge he was more or less in touch with, and often a prominent figure in, the work of the English Society for Psychical Research. After coming to America in 1920 he was for a time a leader in the American Society for Psychical Research in the period when Dr. W. F. Prince was Research Officer. He helped to found the Boston Society for Psychic Research while he was a professor of psychology at Harvard. He was one of those asked by the *Scientific American* to render a verdict on the Boston medium, Margery.

When he came from Oxford to Harvard in 1920, Professor McDougall brought to American psychology a breadth of viewpoint and a degree of courage in attacking a wide field of problems which were unique and somewhat daring. For example, he reintroduced hypnotism to psychologic research. Until he did so, it had been practically abandoned to vaudeville demonstrations. The reader will remember that it was this same fearless pioneer who at Harvard sponsored Murphy and Estabrooks in their attempts to find evidence for telepathy.

Also, he boldly launched a long and painstaking research into a most unpopular theory of evolution. Although by that time biologists had almost all rejected the old hypothesis of Lamarck (which holds that characteristics acquired during the life of the parents may be inherited by the offspring) in favor of other theories more in keeping with the mechanistic trend of the age, he did not hesitate to reopen the question. With groups of rats which he has trained patiently through forty generations and seventeen years of investigation he is convinced that he finds unmistakable evidence that certain training effects are inheritable. He has given his results to science, regardless of the fact that in doing so he stands practically alone in his conclusion.

Further, when Dr. John B. Watson's theory of extreme behaviorism (every human action and emotion is mechanically determined by physical stimuli and automatic nerve patterns, and the mental process as such can be ignored) was so largely narrowing and shadowing the American psychological outlook, Professor McDougall stood out as certainly the leading champion of purposive psychology, which holds that the mind is not only an actual system, but that in its goal-seeking or striving character it causes people to behave as they do. Few laymen would ever suppose otherwise, since the casual efficacy of mind is a common-sense view. But to the behaviorists mind was a fiction, and to many other mechanistic psychologists it was only a reflection or idle accompaniment of nervous activity.

A knowledge of these facts about Professor McDougall goes far to explain the joint investigation of telepathy and clairvoyance by the members of his department. It is the unusual character of his leadership, exerted not in the least as pressure, but rather as inspiration, that largely explains the fact that this work began at Duke and in its department of psychology.

I used the word "inspiration" advisedly. The three of us who constituted his staff had formerly been Dr. McDougall's students, and the natural respect we bore for his views led us to a certain open-mindedness toward his interest in "frontier" topics such as telepathy and clairvoyance. All three recognized these problems as legitimate for investigation without committing ourselves in advance as to what results to expect. The two men who soon had to discontinue the investigation because of pressure of other duties still retain their interested, inquiring attitude toward these phenomena.

There was, therefore, a genuine and unanimous interest on the part of the members of the department. Professor McDougall did not himself institute any actual experimentation; his time was taken up by the Lamarckian experiment, which was at that time already ten years old. But he was always ready to look into the work the rest of us were doing, and throughout has been probably the research's most interested observer. Many times an apropos suggestion or a guiding hand from him has forestalled misfortune. His fifty years of contact with psychic research gave the Duke experiments a background that could not have been found elsewhere. The fact, too, that through his half-century acquaintance with these problems he has kept his scientific poise is of inestimable importance to the dignity of the work. He has always been ready to examine any evidence, but cautious in conclusions. An investigation is enormously favored by having such a sponsor.

3

Associate Professor Helge Lundholm was responsible for the institution of one line of study which, though relatively short-lived, is extremely important in that it was the foundation for later, more successful work. In the fall of 1930, as the result of a discussion with Professor McDougall, he proposed applying tests for telepathic perception to students either in hypnotic trance or after hypnotic treatment designed to put the subject into a favorable state of mind; that is, posthypnotic condition. Dr. Lundholm was himself an experienced hypnotist and had done important research in connection with it. It was understood that I would furnish the techniques for the telepathic testing and Dr. Lundholm would handle the hypnotization. His devotion to the experiments, his patience through the long hours required for the work, and the thoroughness of his handling of the precautions made his withdrawal a real loss when, after several months and with the opening of a new semester, he found that his other work would not permit him to continue.

We began to work on telepathy with hypnotized subjects because the early mesmerists and hypnotists had reported such unique results with them. We thought possibly hypnotization would increase any latent telepathic capacity in a subject and make its demonstration easier. We had heard tales, too, and read accounts of uncanny knowledge of distant events demonstrated by persons in the hypnotic trance, and wondered if these old stories concealed a useful clue.

Our procedure was to begin by putting the subject into a hypnotic trance if we were able. With most of the students who volunteered for the work we found it possible to do so. After some preliminary tests for the adequacy of his trance, the subject was given the suggestion that when he "awakened" he was to get up from his couch, take a certain chair, and follow the instruction he would then receive. He was assured that he would be able to respond to what was in the experimenter's mind without being told what it was. Dr. Lundholm then brought the student out of the trance condition and we proceeded with the tests themselves. In one series of them the subject was asked to tell what number, from 0 to 9, or what letter of the alphabet the experimenter was thinking about. Another test employed a circle divided into eight sections similar to the slices of a pie. The subject, in his posthypnotic condition, placed his finger in the center of the circle and was told to move it to the particular segment of the circumference which the experimenter had mentally selected. We thought that perhaps such a "motor response," or action, might be an easier form of response than speech, but it did not prove to be so.

The results of these experiments in posthypnotic telepathy and clairvoyance were only slightly positive, and at best could be considered merely encouraging. But under the stimulus of that modest encouragement I went on with the work alone for a while after Dr. Lundholm withdrew. Before then I had learned the technique of hypnosis and was still in hopes of finding a subject who would be able to duplicate the feats reported by the early mesmerists.

Working with hypnotism is necessarily a slow business, and the results of our tests had to be constantly checked against similar tests conducted without any hypnotic influence. These nonhypnotic series produced results that were equally good, and fully as encouraging as the ones conducted with posthypnotic subjects. Accordingly I decided not to bother longer with the hypnotic technique, and to this day no one has determined conclusively whether hypnotism is of any service in the investigation of extra-sensory phenomena. We found only that we could get results more quickly without it.

4

At almost the same time that Dr. Lundholm broached the idea of our joint investigation into hypnotism and extra-sensory perception my other colleague, Dr. Karl E. Zener, had become interested in a somewhat different type of work which had come to his attention. This important research had been conducted by a member of the English Society for Psychical Research, Miss Ina Jephson. Miss Jephson had asked her subjects to guess the numbers and suits of ordinary playing cards, and if we accepted the good faith of her subjects and the correct handling of the results, she appeared to have established a good instance of clairvoyance, rather than the telepathy on which we had been working. Like Richet's work with Leonie, her experiments suggested that an *object* might be perceived without using the recognized senses, just as in telepathy there was presumed to be a perception of a *mental image* or state of mind in another person.

I, too, had been interested in Miss Jephson's experiments. I had taken a small part in a repetition of them in co-operation with Dr. Gardner Murphy in New York. Therefore, when Dr. Zener suggested that we repeat Miss Jephson's tests, with some changes, I was again eager to participate. Dr. Zener's experience and personality were especially suitable for co-operation in this work. His training and early research had been in the field of psychology of perception—sensory perception, of course —and he is characteristically a cautious and critical man. His judgment was extremely helpful in the choice of suitable means and methods of testing.

Cards seemed the most convenient sort of object to use in these tests, but the problem of what symbols to put on them had never been settled to our full satisfaction. As a practical solution we decided together on five simple, easily distinguishable designs: a plus or cross, circle, rectangle, star, and three parallel wavy lines.* These figures represented a compromise of the various points that had to be considered.

Our aim, in fact, was to select forms as unlike as possible, even in their parts. We wanted a small enough number of kinds of symbols so that all of them could easily be kept in the subjects' minds. On the other hand, the more we used the greater the advantage of variety.

The cards which Dr. Zener and I devised became far better known than either of us, at that time, could have dreamed. At the start of the work I began calling them "Zener cards," and later on when we changed two of the designs the cards were christened "ESP cards." By that time we were employing the term "extra-sensory perception" (or ESP for short) to describe the clairvoyance and te-

---

* The most recent test cards, designed while this book was in proof, employ a square instead of a rectangle.

TYPES OF TEST CARDS. (TOP) EARLIEST SYMBOLS—THE ZENER CARDS. (BOTTOM) ESP CARDS, 25 IN PACK.

lepathy for which the cards served as a testing technique. It is by this name that they are known today, and the cards of various types which we are now using, and which have been made available to the general public, have been modified and improved from the original designs worked out by Dr. Zener and myself.

At the beginning of our work we did not use the newly devised cards exclusively. We also employed others, such as those containing numbers and letters of the alphabet which Dr. Lundholm and I had used in the hypnosis work. But regardless of the symbols on the particular cards, our method of using them was to seal them all in opaque envelopes and hand them out to students in our classes with an invitation to attempt to name the cards contained in the envelopes. The students were to write down their choices and hand in the record. Many of them were amused, and probably most were politely skeptical. By no means all of them ever carried out the instructions. But among those who did—though there were none who did extremely well—a few had scores which stood out well above the average. On the whole those averages were close to what could be expected from chance or luck alone, but we felt it was worth while to follow up the few individuals who showed exceptional scores. It was in this follow-up that the successful trail was found.

Unfortunately, at this point I was once more to

lose the companionship of a colleague in research. Dr. Zener was too heavily burdened by other work at this time to go on with the decidedly tedious exploration required in the following up of the individual tests. But again a foundation had been laid. A few promising cases had been discovered and something interesting was suggested, if not assured.

5

The fourth member of the psychology staff at Duke was, as the reader already knows, the author of this book. In spite of having a great many other things to do, including a regular, full-time teaching schedule, I did not drop out of the research, and to explain my persistence in it requires a discussion of how I came to be a psychologist and why I happened to be at Duke at this time. So many questions have been asked about the reason for my interest in this work, and how I came to acquire it, that I must answer a few of them with some details of what had preceded my work at Duke.

It was with the definite purpose of undertaking investigation into possible unknown capacities of mind, the so-called psychic powers, that I had first got in touch with Professor McDougall. That was in the early twenties, when he was at Harvard and I was a graduate student in biology at the University of Chicago. My interest in psychic research had grown out of my desire, common, I think, to thousands of people, to find a satisfactory philosophy of life, one that could be regarded as scientifically sound and yet could answer some of the urgent questions regarding the nature of man and his place in the natural world. Dissatisfied with the orthodox religious belief which had at one time impelled me toward the ministry and dissatisfied, except as a last resort, with a materialistic philosophy, I was obviously ready to investigate any challenging fact that might hold possibilities of new insight into human personality and its relations to the universe.

This same interest and curiosity had for a time led me into a broad, restless search along the entire frontier of science and philosophy. I had watched hopefully the efforts of such religious leaders as Shailer Mathews to bring all modern science to the aid of religion. They aimed, with the help of religious-minded scientists, to impress us all so deeply with the great mystery of science itself that we would feel religious about it. This left me cold.

The mysterious capacities claimed for the mind by people engaged in psychic research promised something, at least. The mysteries of the atom or of a distant star could not, at best, have much import for those feelings which once had been religious. But the common claims of psychic research enthusiasts are the very substance of most religious belief, stripped, of course, of theological trappings. The primitives and ancients evidently had relied greatly on the strange occurrences that today would be called psychic in forming their concepts of man, his spiritual make-up, and his powers over nature. I wondered if we were throwing away too much in outgrowing these old beliefs. If some people believed such things were happening today, there was certainly a challenge in looking into them.

When I first learned of the early experiments in thought transference made by Professor (later Sir) Oliver Lodge when he was a young physicist at the University of Liverpool, I asked hopefully, "Might we not find some grounds here for new understanding of ourselves?" The searching mind does not need assurance or certainty, it needs only hope. It was in the sense of following a hope of discovering some illumination—just what, I did not know —that I turned eagerly toward this realm of mysterious happenings, real or imaginary.

A true description of those early years—and the present as well—would begin with my wife, Dr. Louisa Ella Rhine. She is the granddaughter of a German immigrant who was shipwrecked on Sandy Hook, clung to a mast all night, and lived to write a poem about his experience. My wife and I met when we became neighbors in a small Ohio town and studied at the high school there. We used to hold long, juvenile discussions of religion and our philosophical perplexities, and in the course of them became attached to each other. In our college years we studied side by side in the library and the field

and sat together in laboratory and pew. Like myself, she has always been interested in new worlds to
explore, and new roads to travel.

As we grew older and had to decide what to do
with our lives, we turned by common consent to
the field of professional forestry. The woods seemed
to offer a free and natural life, one in which we
might hope to escape the fog of an increasingly
dubious philosophy and work out at least a practical
formula for existence. In preparation for careers in
forestry we became graduate biology students, but
before we had completed our studies in that sphere
our imaginations were caught by the possibilities of
useful work in the borderland science of psychic
research.

The wisdom of meddling with this field seemed to
us at the time highly questionable. My wife fully
shared the questioning as well as the challenge which
this research appeared to offer. Without her I doubt
whether I should have gone ahead, but with her
support and encouragement the decision was easy.

About this time we went to hear Sir Arthur
Conan Doyle give a lecture on spiritualism. I went
with many reservations, almost to scoff, and I left
with the same reservations. But in spite of my
doubts I carried away an impression that I still retain, of what his belief had done to Sir Arthur. It
had made him supremely happy. It had banished
his religious doubts and made him a crusader, willing to make a fool of himself, if necessary, for what

he believed to be a great principle. And clearly if there was a measure of truth in what he believed, misguided though Sir Arthur might be in details, it would be of transcendental importance. This mere possibility was the most exhilarating thought I had had for years.

There is no need to repeat here the psychic adventures, as they are commonly called, through which my wife and I went in the tentative explorations we made. There were years of reading and carefully weighing the literature, of trying to sort out the occasional grain of truth from the unusable chaff that makes up the great part of spiritualistic writing. Explorations among the mediums were discouraging, but they served to sharpen our cautiousness and critical capacities.

Finally an opportunity came to study under Professor McDougall. His books and articles had done much to strengthen our waning interest in the psychic field, and the offer was gratefully accepted. That is how we came to Duke University.

Professor McDougall believed that my background of biological study and research plus my interest in his well-known Lamarckian experiment fitted me to become his research assistant, and he asked me to remain at Duke. In my first year under him, 1927-1928, my wife and I had worked on the criticism and evaluation of the mediumistic material of Dr. John F. Thomas of Detroit, whose studies have now been published under the title

Beyond Normal Cognition. In working on Dr. Thomas's material we had had the advice and supervision of Professor McDougall, and when he asked me to remain with him at Duke it was with the general understanding that I was to have opportunity to carry out such investigation as seemed possible in the special field of the Thomas material—the field of parapsychology.

Psychology is the study of mental life, and parapsychology, as the term is used in this book, is a special branch of psychology. The "para" part of the word might be interpreted as "offside" or "unconventional." The problems of parapsychology are those which, like telepathy, for example, do not appear to fit the conventional view in psychology, but nevertheless seem to many people to have some factual basis. The aim of parapsychology is to find out, first, how sound the facts reported are and, second, to go even further and find new explanations for unusual phenomena of the mind. It differs from psychic research in the strictly experimental methods used in its procedure.

My interest in parapsychology was based largely on this last consideration. Psychic research is conducted, in many cases, on a broad and tolerant approach to unusual mental phenomena. As we have seen, in the earlier discussion of specific cases, it had been difficult, if not impossible, to make it fit into the experimental techniques of the laboratory and the methods of academic teaching. Parapsychology, therefore, was designed for academic study and is today on the curricula of at least three universities.

6

Something of my state of mind in the fall of 1930, after two years at Duke, can be seen from this sketch. The suggestions of my colleagues, Lundholm and Zener, could not, I think, have fallen on more eager ears anywhere on the inhabited globe. The encouragement of their offers to cooperate was the only thing needed to overcome the diffidence I felt in introducing these unconventional problems into university laboratories.

It is clear, too, that several persons played an important part in the setting of the Duke research and that it would in no sense be fair to center whatever recognition may be given it on one individual. The continuation of the work in extra-sensory perception has been marked by this same co-operative spirit. When my colleagues stopped their active cooperation several graduate students of psychology joined me. They did a great share of the work, and an enormous amount of work was done. Two of them are still doing it, and now that their psychological training is complete they are on the permanent staff of the laboratory. Others have gone on to more regular careers in psychology, and new assistants have taken their places.

CHAPTER V

The First High Scoring

THE MONTHS OF WORK WITH ZENER AND LUND-
holm had been marked by one highly interesting
phenomenon. The subjects we were testing for unusual powers of the mind had shown a tendency to
yield the most positive results in spurts of short
duration. Were these flashes of high scoring only
chance occurrences, or was there some principle at
work? There was no immediate way of answering
that question, but the results were encouraging
enough to make us proceed.

It was clear that new methods or conditions of
work were necessary, and the entire spring of that
year was spent in devising them. The problem was
really to track down ways of catching those elusive flashes of extra-sensory perceptiveness which
our subjects had exhibited, and much of the remainder of this book is basically the story of that
pursuit. The successful results from hundreds of
thousands of tests conducted since that time are
due to the finding of effective ways to catch those
transient flashes and registering them objectively so
that they can be weighed and measured and accepted as fact.

The search for conditions which could produce more favorable scores revealed no magic formula. I did not draw upon anything occult or mystical. Instead, the reliance was on much more normal principles, almost on common sense. The first aim was to interest the subjects in the tests, and create confidence in the possibility of doing well. I tried not to test them except when they seemed interested and confident. Scientific ethics required us to count every test we ran, and so every effort was made to create an atmosphere conducive to success. The tests themselves were run as casually and informally as could be, though with adequate safeguard against error. One can easily be cautious without looking like a watchdog. My relations with my subjects were friendly, almost fraternal. We did hypnotic demonstrations, spent long hours in discussion, and pretty completely dissipated the constraints that usually exist for the student in the laboratory and in the presence of his instructor. It seems to me that the sort of relationship created in those laboratory hours is the natural and most wholesome one for instructor and student to maintain in general. At any rate, it is to this relationship that I attribute much of the success that came through the later months of that semester.

2

The casual observer would hardly have been impressed with the dramatic quality of the tests. There

were none of the beakers and retorts which the
chemist sets up on his workbench in complicated
series nor of the intricate and often impressively
powerful pieces of apparatus which the physicist
uses to penetrate the secrets of the atom. Instead,
there were only two men, a table, two chairs, and
a deck of odd-looking cards.

That deck of cards was one of those devised by
Zener and myself and described in the preceding
chapter. It consisted of five cards each of five
"suits" or symbols—a total of 25 cards to the deck.
There were five cards marked with a star, five with
a rectangle, and an equal number with circles,
wavy lines, and pluses or crosses. In other respects
they resembled ordinary playing cards, with uni-
form backs (then blank and later bearing an im-
printed design).

Seated at one side of the table was the subject,
the man or woman who was being tested for extra-
sensory perception. I sat across from him with the
deck of ESP cards, a pencil, and a piece of paper. In
front of me stood the pile of cards, shuffled and
cut. Neither I nor the subject knew the order of
the cards in the deck, any more than the bridge
player knows how an ordinary deck of playing
cards is arranged prior to the deal. The procedure
was simple: the subject tried to name the symbol
on the top card of the deck, which was, of course,
face down. He might stare at the back of the card,
he might be sitting with his eyes closed, or he might

be looking out the window. Sometimes he was allowed to touch the card, but more often not; some of the best subjects did not want to touch them.

After as long a time as he cared to take—usually not more than a few seconds—the subject would name or call what he thought the symbol was on the top card. I would note down his call, remove the top card or let him do so, and we would repeat the procedure with the next card in the deck. Not until we had gone through the entire pack of 25 cards would I look to see whether the subject was calling the symbols correctly. Once we had run through the whole deck, the subject's calls, as noted down on my paper, were checked against the actual order of the cards.

This simple, monotonous procedure seems an almost childish way to investigate the possibility of the human mind's possessing powers not recognized by scientists or the majority of laymen. It lacked every element of drama, employed only one bit of apparatus, a thin deck of cards, and had to be repeated over and over again until subjects had called, through a period of months and years, the symbols on literally millions of cards. And yet, as subsequent pages will make clear, it was a highly satisfactory method of investigation and, ultimately, of proof.

The very simplicity of the technique was an advantage. It reduced the number of possible extraneous factors to a minimum. The results were notably easy to evaluate statistically, and as a method

TELEPATHY CARD TESTING IN THE DUKE LABORATORY.
THE SENDER, BURKE SMITH, IS A STAFF MEMBER.

of work it did not require complicated preliminary training. In the years that followed these first experiments hundreds of investigators were to work with the ESP cards and find them a useful, practicable trail toward new frontiers of psychology.

One more point ought to be made in connection with this working technique. I have indicated it before but it cannot be emphasized too much. Before any card-calling was attempted, every effort was made to interest the subject in the work. I explained the purpose of the tests and how the cards were used. The atmosphere was as informal and as friendly as I could make it. After all, it was a delicate and subtle capacity of the mind for which we were searching, and it was only common sense to try to create an atmosphere favorable to its operation. When the first stiffness and constraint of the subject had been thawed out as far as possible we proceeded to the actual tests. If, after calling through several decks of ESP cards, he failed to score much above the average of 5 right, which luck or chance alone would account for, the tests would be stopped. Sometimes unsuccessful subjects were asked to try again. More often they were not. The successful ones, those whose scores ran consistently above the level of 5 correct calls per deck, were eagerly encouraged and asked to continue with the work. This, too, was common sense, for what we were interested in was not finding out whether *everybody* possesses extra-sensory perceptive powers, but first whether *anybody* does. The problem of how widespread the ESP faculty might be in human beings could not be considered until we had proved its existence and discovered ways to establish and test it.

It is easy to confuse a method with its results. Our card method of research was a useful tool, but there was nothing intrinsically important about it beyond the fact that it did prove practical. Far more important than the cards themselves, I believe, or the statistical appraisal which they made possible was the way in which the tests were conducted. Not what was done, but the way in which it was done contributed most to the results. The cards did not develop a new faculty of the mind—they merely recorded an existing faculty in a simple, practical way. The atmosphere which led the subjects to an eager and interested frame of mind was the vital factor. The subjects caught the spirit of what was presented to them as a game, so to speak, and probably any investigator in this field who will go to the trouble of inspiring keen, spontaneous interest in his subjects will be successful with this card technique or with others.

3

The tests for clairvoyance, made in the spring of 1931, began to give indication that the research was on the right track. It is important to understand plainly in what way these tests did indicate some form of extra-sensory perception, and the explanation of how they did so involves a certain amount of simple mathematics. That spring the subjects made 800 trials or individual calls. That is, they indicated their impressions of the symbols on 800 cards, face down before them. The average for *all* the subjects tested, and for every one of the individual calls, was 6½ correct out of each group of 25.

Is there anything significant in that *average*? That depends on whether or not you know how to appraise it. Neither my colleagues nor I had any expectation that we should find subjects who could call *all* the cards right every single time. What we were looking for was subjects who could accurately name more cards than mere chance could account for. A partial analogy might be drawn from business, where the purpose is not to make a clear 100 per cent profit on every transaction, but to show a percentage of profit on the entire number. If a businessman succeeds in doing that he is getting results in his particular field. The results of our tests demonstrated much the same sort of "profit" or gain over the scores which could have been expected—and accurately predicted—if chance alone were operating in the calls made by our subjects.

How does a score, an average score, of 6½ cards correctly named in each group of 25 prove that something more than sheer chance or luck was operating in those tests in the Duke laboratory? To answer that question it is necessary to know just what score chance alone would give in the same series of tests carried out mechanically, that is, by excluding the possibility of any sort of human extra-sensory perception. Fortunately, there are several ways of finding out what the score would have been if sheer chance had been operative. We can employ logic to find out, or we can make actual tests, trial demonstrations, or we can consult the authority of those who are expert in the laws of chance. The simplest of these methods to apply at the start of this explanation is logic.

Everyone knows that if I put five different cards face down on the table, each with one of the numbers from 1 to 5 on its face, and ask someone to guess the number on a designated card, the chance is 1 in 5 that he will guess correctly, or "score a hit," if he has no way of knowing which is which. Now, if I tell him whether he is right or not and then ask him to guess another specified card, the chance of hitting changes at once in his favor. But if I do not tell him whether he hit or missed on the first guess (and in our work we do not), he knows no more on the second guess than he did on the first one; consequently, the chances are the same as before. He may think he knows the first card guessed if he believes strongly in his ESP ability; but if we assume there is no ESP, then his belief could have no foundation, and any conclusion based on a mere unfounded belief could not help him at all in guessing the other cards.

Accordingly, if I do not tell him whether he is right or wrong, he can go on until he guesses all five cards, and even with the fifth there is still the same chance of hitting as at first. For the subject has learned nothing that can reliably guide his guessing on the fifth. I have often had long arguments with persons interested in this point, but none has ever accepted my challenge to gamble with me, putting odds of more than 1 in 5 on the fifth card.

The same principle holds, of course, for the tenth card or the twenty-fifth, if there is a pack instead of five. If the chance is 1 in 5 for success on each card clear through the whole pack, this means that it is 5 in 25, 20 in 100, or 200 in 1,000 trials. This is the number most to be expected, or *the mean chance expectation*. In the long run the average would closely approximate this figure.

Put the matter to actual test and you will get the same result, or one only an insignificant fraction different. It is easy to try it out. Take two packs of cards and pretend that one of them represents the guesses or calls of a subject. Match these decks against each other and note down the number of times cards at the same respective points in the two decks happen to coincide. These "hits" are the result of pure chance. They may total exactly 5, or more often a number above or below that figure. Shuffle both decks and match them again and again, as long as you have the patience to keep it up. You ought to match them at least 100 times before you can feel that you have given the question a scientifically satisfactory test. Next, add up the total number of hits and divide that figure by the total number of runs. The result will give you the average number of hits per run. The more runs you make the more likely will this figure approach an even 5.0.

Competent investigators actually have matched hundreds of thousands of cards in this and similar ways, and the results are always close to chance—5 right out of every 25 cards—and never as high as the average of 6.5 right which our early ESP investigations produced.

Once we had determined what average to expect from chance factors alone we were able to discover *how much* our actual results were beyond or above chance. All we had to do was to subtract the chance expectation from the actual scores made by our subjects; the difference between the two figures gave us what is called *deviation*. In our 800 trials chance alone could be expected to yield one-fifth that many hits, or a total of 160. But the actual number of our subjects' hits was 207—47 more hits than chance would be expected to produce.

Perhaps a deviation of 47 hits in this case was nothing to marvel at. Might that deviation itself not be the result of chance? How sure could we be that such was not the case?

The answers to these questions do not make light and easy reading. It is not possible to write about mathematical computations in quite the same language in which a good story is told, and many readers may wish to spare themselves the tedium of the next paragraphs, though there is nothing about them, I hope, which the ordinary reader will not be able to understand. If you care to skip the less exciting part of this chapter, then, turn ahead to the next section, which is numbered 4.

In the statistical analysis which our research employs it is necessary to have a way of telling what variations in chance scores may occur, and how often they may be looked for. A truly chance series rarely averages exactly 5.0, although the average in a long run is seldom far from it. Fortunately, it is mathematically possible to find out how often to expect a deviation as great as 47 in 800, and the answer is expressed in terms of once in a hundred series of the same size, or once in a thousand or a million such series. Mathematicians have worked out a standard formula for determining the odds against chance as the cause of deviation.

A full explanation of how that formula was derived and how it is applied to the results of ESP tests would require lengthy discussion before it could be fully understood.* The general idea, however, is simple enough. Given a series of trials— say 800—with a deviation of 47 from the mean or ordinary chance expectation, how unlikely is it that this deviation itself occurred by chance? If, for instance, the odds should be only 10 to 1 against chance, scientists feel that it is not sufficiently unlikely to be beyond the range of accidental occurrence, and hence they prefer odds of 100 or 150 to 1. Such odds as these are consistently relied upon in scientific work as a basis for further investigation.

Even so, in our laboratory no important conclusion is based upon such low odds as 150 to 1. Nothing less than odds of thousands to one is acceptable as proof of any point of importance, and the actual figures give odds of millions and upward to one.

The yardsticks most often used in measuring deviation from chance are the *probable error* (PE) and the *standard deviation* (SD), though the former is seldom used in this work today. The standard deviation method involves selecting mathematically the deviation from chance for the particular series at which the odds are 1 in 3 that such a deviation is itself due to chance. The actual experimental deviation established by the tests is then divided by this

* The reader who is seriously interested in going further into this point may wish to consult G. Irving Gavett's *Statistical Method*, R. A. Fisher's *Statistical Methods for Research Workers*, or Thornton Fry's *Probability and Its Engineering Uses*. More detailed and thorough treatment of the mathematics of probability as applied to this type of research appears in current numbers of the *Journal of Parapsychology*.

new hypothetical deviation to produce a critical ratio, or expression in numerical terms of how unlikely it is that actual deviation is the result of chance.

The standard deviation is arrived at by multiplying together the number of trials, the chance of getting a hit, and the chance of a miss, and simply taking the square root of the product. If the probability of getting a hit on any one particular trial is 1 in 5, or 1/5, the probability of making a miss is naturally 4 in 5, or 4/5. To apply the principle to our 800 trials, then, multiply 800, 1/5, and 4/5 and extract the square root. This gives a standard deviation for the whole number of trials as 11.3. Since our tests had produced an experimental deviation of 47, we divide that figure by the standard deviation and get a result of 4.2, which means that there was only one chance in about 250,000 that our results could be attributed to purely chance factors. Such odds amount practically to certainty, and no one in science or out of it ought to ask for more than that!

This yardstick, the standard deviation, is a curiously elastic one. It varies to fit the total number of runs against which it is applied, being larger for long series and smaller for short series. In other words, if the 47 hits over and above chance about which we have been talking had been the result of 8,000 trials instead of 800, we should have divided the deviation of 47 by a different standard deviation.

In case 8,000 trials were to produce no more than 47 hits above the level of chance, this deviation would not have been a *significant* one because the larger number of trials would allow more room for chance alone to produce such a deviation.

On the other hand, while an experimentally derived deviation of 47 means more in a short series than it does in a long one, the *average* of 6.5 hits per 25 cards which our subjects had been scoring would be more and more significant the longer the series. By continuing at that level there would be an ever-increasing deviation, one less and less likely to happen as the result of pure chance.

This sounds a little complicated perhaps, but it can more easily be expressed in terms of a simple table which will show the entire relationship and at the same time give some figures for significant deviations. The first, or left-hand, column here takes certain *averages* of hits per 25 cards, beginning as low as 5.25 and running up to 11.0. The second column gives the number of runs which would have to be made *at the specified average* before the deviation could be considered significant. If chance alone would not account for this deviation more than once in 150 times, it is considered significant. (You can easily understand that if the odds against a certain result are 150 to 1 in the case of a short series, such as 25 trials, that one chance is more likely to occur than when, in the case of a longer series, such as 250 trials, the odds against

a certain result are the same. That is, once in 150
times 250 is a much smaller chance than once in 150
times 25. That is why we rarely use the measure
of the standard deviation on series of fewer than
200 trials, and never on those below 100.) Column
three of the table gives the number of actual hits
a subject has to make in the given number of runs
in order to score the average given in the first
column and accumulate an experimental deviation
—or total hits above mean chance—of 2½ times
our standard deviation yardstick. The number of
hits above mean chance level required to do this in
a ratio of 1 in 150 is given in the last column.

Average number of hits per run of 25	Number of runs of 25 trials	Total of hits required for significance	Actual deviation which is 2½ times standard deviation
5.25	400	2100	100
5.50	100	550	50
6.00	25	150	25
6.50	12	78	18
6.80	8	55	15
7.00	7	49	14
7.50	4	30	10
8.00	3	24	9
9.00	2	18	8
11.00	1	11	6

Even if the explanation before this table has not
made the complicated business of probability entirely clear to you, it will show you that the fewer
runs a subject makes, the more hits he has to score
to prove beyond reasonable doubt that he is perceiving extra-sensorily. On very long runs only a small
average above what we should expect from chance
proves the point more conclusively than a larger

average on a smaller number of runs. As I have said, we never base conclusions on results that involve series shorter than 8 runs or 200 trials.

4

One thing, at least, must be clear by this time. My casual-appearing explorations were producing averages that were not due to chance. I felt greatly encouraged to continue the quest, though it was slow and laborious. I have already explained how much of an effort was made to put the subject at his ease and awake an interest in the tests before they were given. There was no way of telling just how much of this intangible, personal preparation was necessary for the results I was getting, and I did not dare take a chance on lowering those results by attempting any short cuts.

Then there was the question of scientific precaution. We were exploring an unknown process of the mind, and the first thing our successful tests had to do was to convince me and my colleagues of their objective validity. So we took a wide range of precautions. Six or more packs of cards were kept at hand and the test pack changed frequently. In this way new packs were introduced, cards which had never been seen before by the subjects using them. We were careful not to allow an opportunity of studying the backs of the cards, in order to prevent the possibility of any of the students with whom we were working being able to distinguish the cards by almost microscopic markings on their backs. Such small markings may appear as a result of handling, but as soon as the cards showed signs of wear and tear they were discarded. Care was exercised to have the card called before it was removed from the deck and all shiny tabletops covered or avoided so that there would be no reflection when the pack was cut. The check-up was made a double-observation affair, both experimenter and subject seeing both card and record and score. Later we adopted several further protective devices such as screens and distance. All these precautions, and others, will be discussed again in the chapters where they most naturally belong.

Indeed, we went so slowly at this time that we rarely asked a subject to call more than 25 cards in any one day. The principal result of our tests that spring was not the average of 6.5 hits out of 25, but an understanding of the way in which to conduct the tests themselves in order to make positive results possible.

5

The academic year was drawing to a close, and though the results of the tests I had conducted were favorable enough to encourage me and to warrant carrying on the research, I had not yet come upon a subject with a startling capacity for extra-sensory perception. Yet all the time there was

such a person close at hand. It was almost by accident that he was discovered. His name was A. J.
Linzmayer, and he was actually one of our own
undergraduate students in psychology. When Dr.
Zener and I had tested a class of more than a hundred students, Linzmayer had turned in the best
score of the group, but he had not done unusually
well in the few subsequent individual tests we had
given him, and consequently little work had been
done with him as a subject. His ability would probably never have been discovered if it had not been
for his interest in hypnotism.

One day late in the month of May he dropped
in at the laboratory, and I made a relatively unsuccessful attempt to hypnotize him. While he was
still lying on a couch in the laboratory I picked up
a pack of ESP cards and shuffled them. Almost
everyone who came my way in those days was asked
to try at least a run or two of the cards. Standing
at the window, well out of Linzmayer's line of
vision, I glanced at a card and asked him what it
was. He told me, correctly. Glancing at the next
card, I held it under my hand so that it would be
completely out of the question for him to see it,
even if he happened to look my way, and asked him
again what it was. He told me, again correctly. In
fact, he called *nine* cards in succession correctly.

Here was something amazing! The mathematical
odds against accurately calling nine cards in a row
are in the neighborhood of two million to one—

5 to the ninth power. No such result as that has
ever occurred in all the tests which have been conducted to determine the mathematics of pure
chance.

The next day Linzmayer again made a run of
9 straight accurate calls, and I realized that here
was a subject who had what amounted to a genius
for extra-sensory perceptivity. My excitement at
the discovery was doubtless highly unbecoming in
a scientist and I could not help communicating a
good deal of it to Linzmayer. Neither of us could
believe that two runs of 9 straight hits, made
on successive days and by the same man, were due
to any imaginable chance or luck. The odds against
that explanation for the two runs together were
astronomical, and it would have been stretching
skepticism to the point of folly to assign any chance
cause to them. Something was working here which
was real enough to produce results, however far
it might be outside the border of accepted thought
and belief.

These runs of 9 straight hits were the most
sensational made up to that time, though later experiments were to produce far more impressive
ones. Both of us became excited, and as we continued with the testing Linzmayer's scores began to
drop. When we finally stopped, after calling 300
cards, his last scores were at the level of chance,
or 5 correct out of 25. But for the series as a whole
he had averaged almost twice what chance alone

could have been expected to produce. Instead of 60 right out of 300 calls, Linzmayer had named 119 cards correctly.

The day after his second series of nine hits in a row was to have been Linzmayer's last at Duke. He had made arrangements to drive home with a friend, and a summer job was waiting at the other end of the trip. He needed the money, and our research could not take the responsibility of asking him to stay longer. In a most generous and co-operative spirit he promised to let us have every possible hour of his last day, and we made plans to utilize the time to the best advantage. What we most needed from him, of course, was the largest possible number of significant scores, but this kind of work could not be rushed. The moment I tried to hurry him his scores dropped, and certainly against his own will to succeed. He was willing to try any condition of testing we wanted, but the gift we were trying to measure was apparently in great part beyond his control.

Linzmayer had a theory that he could do his best work if he made his runs while looking out the window. He thought that this slight diversion kept him from getting fixed mental habits about calling the order of the cards. On the morning of his last day, accordingly, we started off the tests with Linzmayer standing at the window of the laboratory on the top floor of the Duke Medical Building and looking across the treetops.

For a while this arrangement gave us good results, but finally we decided that it did not offer enough distraction to keep the work from getting monotonous. I suggested going for a ride in my car to give him a change of attention. My plan was to stop after a time in some quiet place and do another test or two. Then we could go on to another, and a third, as long as the method seemed to be effective.

For some time we drove along quietly. Then it occurred to me to test my subject on the way to the place where I had planned to make our first stop. I pulled the car up at the side of the road but did not bother to turn off the engine. Putting a large notebook across Linzmayer's knees, I took a pack of ESP cards out of my pocket and held it in my hand. He, meantime, had leaned back with his head resting against the top of the seat, so that his eyes saw nothing but the roof of the car. There were no mirrors or shiny surfaces into which he could have looked for possible reflections. During the actual progress of the test, his eyes were closed.

After giving the pack a cut—neither of us knew the order of the cards in it anyway—I drew off the top one and tipped it toward me just enough to catch a glimpse of the symbol and then put it face down on the notebook on Linzmayer's lap. Without looking at it or touching it he said, after a pause of about two seconds:

"Circle."

"Right," I told him, drew off the next card, and laid it on the notebook.

"Plus," he said.

"Right."

"Waves."

"Right."

"Waves."

"Right."

At this point I shuffled the deck again, cut it once more, and again drew off a card.

"Star," Linzmayer said when the card was placed on the notebook. It was a star.

When he had called *fifteen cards in succession* without a single mistake, both of us were too amazed for a while to go on with the rest of the run. No conceivable deviation from probability, no "streak of luck" which either of us had ever heard of could parallel such a sequence of unbroken hits. We both knew that the thing Linzmayer had just done was virtually impossible by all the rules in the book of chance, but he had done it.

Eventually we went on with the run, and in the final 10 cards of that series Linzmayer made 6 hits. His total was 21 correct calls out of a possible 25. It is hard to express the remoteness of the possibility that Linzmayer had got his results by pure chance. Merely to indicate the odds against that initial series of 15 successive accurate calls having a chance explanation requires a ratio of 1 to something over 30,000,000,000, and the score of

21 out of 25 would produce an even greater one. On paper and in print such figures mean nothing concrete to the ordinary person. They are astronomically large, and we did not consider them seriously for a moment; we both knew that we were on the threshold of a proof for the existence of extra-sensory perception which would be able to satisfy even the most skeptical.

No reader of this book need consider the account of this extraordinary run of Linzmayer's as presumptive evidence that ESP is a fact. The conditions of the test were not our usual laboratory ones, and the scientific evidence for ESP rests upon work performed under the strictest conditions. Write that amazing score off, if you like, to mere exploration. With all the skepticism I can muster, though, I still do not see how any sensory cue could have revealed to Linzmayer the symbols of those 21 cards he called correctly.

We spent the rest of the day together driving along country roads or in the Duke forest, stopping to make one test run of the cards after another. The occasional passers-by must have thought us a very unusual couple of men indeed, with one of us sitting with his eyes shut or fixed on the sky and his back turned upon his companion, who was picking up little cards one at a time and apparently making a record every time the first man spoke a word.

6

It is difficult for people who are not familiar
with the methods of scientific research to appreciate the value of negative results. Yet they are as
important in their way as positive ones; it is essential to know what a thing is *not,* to learn the circumstances which will exclude it from the picture,
so to speak, as well as those which will produce it.
In the research with Linzmayer, then, it was important to find out if his gift for extra-sensory
perceptivity could be rendered inoperative. In
learning the factors which would affect it adversely
we should be finding out something positive about
its nature.

Already the creation of a favorable atmosphere
for the subject has been stressed, and in studying the
methods of doing so I had noticed that one of the
worst things I could do was to press the subject,
either to take the test when he was reluctant or to
call the cards under conditions which did not appeal to him. This discovery agreed with the work
of earlier investigators. Richet, in his tests, had
found that long, fatiguing runs lowered his subjects' scoring, and Estabrooks had noticed that even
in so short a run as twenty cards the larger number of correct calls was likely to lie in the first ten.
H. L. Frick, one of my students who had been doing ESP work, confirmed these findings by long

runs of 100, in which, toward the end, he tended
to go below the chance average.

Clearly the next step was to find out what would
happen to Linzmayer if he was hurried and asked to
work under pressure and against his will. Previous
experience and logic suggested that his scores ought
to show a marked drop, but it was important to
verify this hypothesis by actual experiment. So,
without explaining what was behind the request, I
urged him to stay on and work a little longer and
past the time when we had agreed to stop. I altered
my manner toward him, demanding that he go
faster and try to squeeze in a greater number of
runs in the same space of time. In the few additional hours which he was courteous enough to
grant he made half again as many trials as in the
several preceding days. But where, in the 600
former trials he had averaged 10 right calls for
each deck of 25 cards, in the first 500 trials under
pressure he dropped to an average of 4, and in the
next 400 his average was almost precisely the chance
expectation of 5 per 25.

These results were in line with our expectation.
With the same tools—the cards—and in conditions
which were physically unchanged, by applying
pressure and doing things in a way which I knew
to be wrong, we had been able to get a new series
against which to check the earlier one, a series in
which the results were no better than chance itself

would have produced, and in fact below the chance average. Linzmayer himself wished to score high, as before, but the conditions under which his last series of calls were made had prevented him from doing so. Indeed, the less-than-chance average suggested the possibility of creating a negative block of some sort in the mental path of the extra-sensory process.

7

The loss of Linzmayer as a subject handicapped a research which was small in personnel and without any real financial resource. Here and there, however, we were able to find a promising subject, enlisting the interest of a number of students in the search for a second Linzmayer. Most active among them was an able student of mathematics, Charles E. Stuart. He had been in one of my classes earlier and had been a subject in the experiments conducted by Lundholm and myself. Stuart had given some promise of extra-sensory perceptivity, though not a great deal. But he instituted an investigation of his own in the dormitory, mainly with his fraternity brothers: using a pack of cards slightly different from those which Zener and I had designed, he conducted a large number of tests on those of his friends whom he could interest. The results were even higher than my own. This gave me the first independent illustration of what has since become almost a recognized rule: the less formid-

HUBERT PEARCE, ON THE LEFT, CALLING DOWN
THROUGH A PACK OF ESP CARDS. PROFESSOR RHINE IS
RECORDING HIS CALLS.

able the investigator and the more friendly and
casually he can be taken by the subjects, the better the results are likely to be. This is the reason why
much of the best work in the subsequent stages of
this investigation is, and has been, going on in the
hands of responsible undergraduate investigators
who are supervised and sponsored by staff members.

Stuart's work seemed to be well done and carefully recorded, so far as I could judge. In fact, it
made such an impression on me that I resolved to
encourage him as far as was possible to continue in
this field of research. I am happy to say that he is
now my colleague on the staff of the Parapsychology Laboratory.

But it was with himself as subject that Stuart
did his most remarkable work. If one wishes, he
may completely reject this work as not being done
in good faith, but it does seem to possess all the ear-
marks of genuineness. I am sure that no one who
has known Stuart at the university would consider
any question of his honesty reasonable. Besides, he
has since been tested by other investigators, and
the results have well borne out the capacities
demonstrated in the work he did alone.

The characteristic thing about Stuart's scoring
is that it begins well, but declines after a time. The
first period of his work lasted through several
months, and began with an average of 9 hits per
25. Then the scores gradually came down to chance
through a series of 7,500 trials. Later he resumed

work and set out with an average beyond 7 hits per 25. Again the scores dropped off to chance after 2,000 trials. Since then he has shown other spurts of ability when a new and challenging situation has arisen, but the period of his effective scoring has grown relatively shorter with each turn.

In the progressive declines manifested by Stuart's work we have learned something about the strange phenomenon which it helped to demonstrate. We have learned that this ability is something that plays out when the original novelty wears off and is re-aroused when a fresh attack with renewed interest is made; Stuart seldom fails to respond with above-chance scores to the challenge of a new technique. In addition, then, to merely piling up more evidence for ESP in Stuart's work, we were getting at some of its elementary relationships to other psychological principles.

8

While Stuart was carrying out his work, my attention was primarily engaged with Linzmayer again. Through a small grant from the university we were able to finance a week's visit from him in the fall of 1931. He had lost something, but I seriously doubt that this was due to the mistreatment of those last few hours' work in the spring. More probably it was because he now had a reputation to live up to and could not avoid being under a certain amount of strain. He was being modestly paid to do the work, and it is likely that much of the spontaneity of the original experiment was gone. That had been adventure. This was work.

In spite of various devices for enlivening the experiments, I could not get him to score above an average of 6.5. But each experimental series with Linzmayer—eventually, four in all—was highly significant of something beyond chance, in spite of the declining average scores. As the scores fell off, more trials were made. On a second visit in the spring of 1932 he could do little better, averaging 6.7. Finally, in 1933, his fourth experimental period, he was down to 5.9. Even this low average, in the 3,000 trials made during that period, is significant of something beyond chance. Linzmayer's decline reinforced what we learned from our work with Stuart.

Another test which we made with Linzmayer in March of 1932 proved to be an important one, and though it may appear somewhat unusual, it was actually one of the recognized methods of psychologic investigation. In tests for the different mental processes which psychologists study it is important to try out the effects of fatigue, drugs, and anything else which may influence them. We had already discovered that pressure and fatigue tended to lower a subject's ability at ESP, and we decided next to try, with every precaution, the effect of a non-habit-forming narcotic drug.

Sodium amytal was selected because of its safety, and we gave Linzmayer a dose of it one day. In the runs he had been making just before we gave him the drug his scores had been averaging 6.8; after taking the first dose, no effect upon him was observable, even within the proper allowance of time. We had interrupted the testing until we were sure that the sodium amytal was working, and were looking for signs of "dissociation" or intoxication, such as inco-ordination, dizziness, and drowsiness. Linzmayer was a strong young man in perfect health, and he playfully resisted the action of the drug, insisting that it had not affected him. After a half hour we gave him a second dose, and finally a third, before he began to exhibit the normal effects of a narcotic. By the time it had taken full effect he was decidedly drowsy and behaved a good deal like a moderately drunken man. His tongue was thick and his speech somewhat incoherent. He was talkative and frank, and had trouble in walking straight. In general his judgment was impaired, but he was able to see, hear, and feel as much as a normal man. His *sensory* perception, in other words, was still functioning, while the higher processes which normally direct the senses were confused. What, then, of extra-sensory perception?

In this condition, Linzmayer's ability to score in the tests for *extra*-sensory perception was completely gone, and his average came down to 5.0.

I worked him as long as I could keep him awake. He did not want to sit up, and when he lay down it was almost impossible to keep him from sleeping. Obviously extra-sensory perception was completely inhibited long before sensory perception gave out and the subject went to sleep. Here was a clear relationship, though a negative one, which discriminated extra-sensory from sensory perception, and similar tests with later subjects and smaller doses directly confirmed it.

A narcotic drug which interferes with nervous action also interferes with ESP. It indicates that the nervous system is involved in some phase of extra-sensory perception at least as we are testing it.

Such research is never free from a personal and sometimes amusing side. For instance, there I was alone with Linzmayer, who was heavily and, to the superficial eye, drunkenly asleep. I had not expected to have to dose him so heavily and had made no provision for the outcome. It would be unwise to attract attention by calling for help, because explanation at such a time is difficult. Work in our field is best done quietly—certainly so on a college campus. What could I do? Linzmayer was staying in one of the dormitories, and it was broad daylight. By hammering the soles of his feet to waken him, and by challenging him, I managed to get him to attempt to walk. Smuggling him down an elevator to a back exit, I succeeded in getting him into my car, where he at once sprawled across the back seat and fell into a deep sleep even before I got the car started.

For a time I drove my human "guinea pig" around the countryside in the hope that the fresh air blowing over him would revive him. In the end I took him to my home and managed to get him awake long enough to drink two cups of strong coffee. When I returned to the car he had fallen into as deep a sleep as ever. Not wishing to have to explain his absence, and disclose my research prematurely to campus curiosity, I headed back to the dormitory and pulled up to the back door of the building, where I managed to shake him into half wakefulness, and with his arm over my shoulder we paraded down the hallway to his room while the students were all at supper. I left him under a cold shower, thinking that by this time the major effect of the drug might well be supposed to be over. At any rate he could go to bed and "sleep it off." I was enormously relieved, Linzmayer was none the worse for the experience, and he had contributed something important to the research.

One more circumstance helped to increase our growing confidence and enthusiasm. By the end of the academic year of 1931-1932 we had been able to find a number of other people besides Linzmayer and Stuart who were able to demonstrate a positive capacity for extra-sensory perception. There were now at least a dozen of them, though none so brilliant as the two men whose work has been described in this chapter, and we began to feel that they were not simply fortunate discoveries. If ESP subjects were relatively easy to find it would make our research that much easier to carry on, and at this stage none of us would have considered for a minute the idea of not going on with the work.

CHAPTER VI

Further Advances

IN THE SEVEN YEARS OF THE DUKE EXPERIMENTS,
our most important discovery so far as subjects
were concerned was a young man named Hubert
Pearce. He proved to be probably the best subject
discovered in all the research on extra-sensory perception. Finding him was not merely a happy accident.

One day in the early spring of 1932 I delivered
a talk to the students of the Duke School of
Religion, describing the work in parapsychology.
After it was over, a young divinity student who had
been in the audience came to me to say that he was
specially interested in our experiments because of
certain psychic experiences that had occurred in
his family. His mother, he told me, had possessed
psychic capacities, and he had been a witness to
some impressive demonstrations of them.

"Do you possess some of these capacities yourself?" I asked him.

"Yes," he said, "but I am afraid of them."

I assured him that there was nothing to fear from
exercising his special perceptive powers under controlled conditions and in a laboratory. So he agreed

to take some tests. I asked him to report to J. G. Pratt, who had already begun to carry on a considerable part of the research.

Almost from the beginning Pearce showed marked ability in the card-calling tests. In fact, in the course of the first 100 trials it was evident that here was an exceptional scorer. On the first 5,000 trials he averaged close to 10 hits out of 25. Day in and day out for two years his scores could be relied upon to average around that figure. Sometimes they went higher for a day and sometimes lower, but always they were above the chance average. We constantly wanted more work from him than his schedule would permit his giving us.

Pearce turned out to be just the man we needed for exploration into the nature of extra-sensory perception. A great share of what we have discovered by way of important ESP relationships came from the work done with him. Of course most of it was confirmed in the work of others, but he was so adaptable to changes in working conditions and so willing to adjust himself to new demands that we made greater progress with him than we had ever been able to do before we found him.

Pearce was a man of slight build, somewhat nervous and sensitive, and tremendously interested in doing good scoring. Failure affected him deeply. When everything was going well he was happy in his accomplishments and seemed to enjoy the work as much as any of us. He appreciated the importance of what he was doing and felt that it was not unrelated to the fundamentals of his religious calling.

Although his attitude was always co-operative and he never refused to try anything that was proposed to him, we soon found that it was better for him to suggest changes in technique or procedure, or at least to let him take a part in helping to decide them. Apparently it was a question of getting co-operation from a part of his personality over which he did not have full conscious control. For instance, when he himself suggested that he call right down through a pack of cards without removing one—a proposal which at the time was made almost in the spirit of a boast—he had no difficulty in so doing and making an excellent score. But when I suggested the slight change that he divide the pack into piles of five each and call them he did not succeed.

At one time we wanted to run some tests with a special deck of ESP cards carrying very small symbols. The purpose was to find out whether the size of the symbols affected the subject's ability to perceive them extra-sensorily, and we used symbols so small that they averaged only about three millimeters in diameter. By arranging to have the suggestion for this test come through Pearce himself his confidence was unshaken and he succeeded in scoring just as well with these minute symbols as with the regular cards. Later on there will be a

good deal to say about certain tests which we conducted at a distance, and in this case, too, we succeeded in inducing Pearce to propose the work to
us instead of the other way round.

Pearce was not a sensational scorer. He seldom
made long perfect runs, but his results displayed a
sort of rhythm. An analysis of his scores reveals a
number of internal curves which are similar to
those produced by other mental performances, such
as a memory test, which are much better understood than ESP. For instance, he did better toward
the beginning and end of a run than in the middle.
The average person is likely to show the same tendency whether it is a case of a run of ESP cards or
memorizing a poem. Most of us have noticed that
it is easier to remember the first and last stanzas
of a poem; or, in a column of figures, the first five
and the last five. Certainly it was normal to expect
Pearce to do better in the first five and the last
five cards of a run. Many other subjects have since
displayed the same scoring pattern, and it is important because it helps to relate extra-sensory perception to the other processes of mind and contributes
something toward its understanding.

2

Runs like those of Linzmayer—9 and 15 successive hits—did not appear in Pearce's work. There

is one dazzling exception to this rule, though, and it is worth a story in itself.

One day when I was working alone in the laboratory Pearce came by, not intending to take any tests. He had no appointment with me, but I asked him if he wanted to do a little extra work. He answered that he had an engagement elsewhere. Remembering the Linzmayer episode in which I had used pressure and insisted upon working, even against the subject's evident desire, I asked Pearce to try just a few calls. I picked up the pack of cards with which I had been compiling a checkup on the laws of chance and asked him to call the top card. After he called five wrong in succession, which was unusual for him, I began joking with him as to where he was probably going and commented that he must be very anxious indeed to get there, as evidenced by his score. Stirred by my teasing, or perhaps by accident, he got three hits in the next five cards. I felt then that he was definitely responding to this unusual approach and I intensified the challenge.

"I'll bet a hundred dollars you can't get this one," I said banteringly.

He did.

"Another hundred on this one," I told him.

He got that card right too. I kept up my ruinous betting and he kept on winning until he completed 25 hits in unbroken succession. As the cards were

called and observed, they were returned to the pack
and a cut made each time. Ordinarily in our tests
the card would not be looked at until the end of
a run of 25 and was not returned to the pack. But
this case was exceptional in every way. As Pearce
called the twenty-fifth card correctly there was a
definite break of tension in both of us. We declared
a halt by mutual consent.

Pearce's calling 25 cards in a row correctly was
the most phenomenal thing that I have ever observed. If there is anyone in the world who can
believe that it was due to sheer luck, that would
be another phenomenon almost equally startling.
The odds against his feat having been due to pure
and undiluted chance are 1 in 298,023,223,876,-
953,125. The size of this figure is not intended to
stun the reader into believing in extra-sensory perception on the spot, but to express, in this single
case, just how unlikely it is that luck could account
for that sequence of unbroken hits.

In this particular series I held the cards myself;
most of the time, as was his custom in making calls,
Pearce did not even glance at them. In fact, he had
not touched the pack of cards since coming into
the laboratory. He did not even sit down or take
off his topcoat.

When it was over, Pearce spontaneously said,
"Well, you'll never get me to do that again!"

"Why?" I asked. "You seemed to do it easily
enough."

"Well, I don't know, but you will never get me to do it again."

That was all he could say in explanation of his feelings. It was not that he was tired. The test had not hurt him. The most one can infer with safety is that anxiety not to miss each next call was a constant, cumulative strain upon him, just as it would have been in the case of any performance where scoring on individual trials was important and a perfect record the ultimate goal. We never did get Pearce to do it again. For that matter, there never was another situation as unique, one in which there was an opportunity to challenge him without being taken too seriously. On the other hand, he may have considered subconsciously that it would require unusual effort to repeat such a run, and since he had already done it once, what adequate point was there in doing it again? (The reader may wonder whether Pearce ever collected his $2,500. I need only say that the sum approaches an average college professor's yearly salary, which ought to be a satisfactory reply.)

The levity of the situation was more important than the money. In fact, the few times I have seriously offered a money reward to subjects for good scoring have not been successful. The subjects themselves protest that such rewards interfere. I doubt if this would be true for every subject, but the students who were working in our laboratory had, on the whole, sufficient motivation, and money would have been a distraction. Some of them, although they needed money badly, would not accept the hourly wage which subjects were offered as a routine to justify our demanding so much of their time. Their interest in the work itself or their friendship for the experimenter, which I acknowledge most gratefully, furnished the main motivation both for most of the assistant experimenters and for the subjects themselves.

3

From this point on, the story of our work with Pearce is so intimately bound up with the many ramifications of the entire research that it will be best to reserve most of it for future chapters and tell here only what happened in the end to his career as an ESP subject. I had been fearing and expecting some sort of denouement; the history of other good subjects had already warned me that sooner or later something was likely to go wrong with his scoring ability. Most of the subjects with whom other investigators had worked, provided that they did so long enough, had come to an end of the ability to demonstrate their special powers. There was the early case of the Creery sisters, mentioned in the third chapter of this book. Richet's prize subject, Leonie, declined in her results, as did Brugmans's good subject. Unfortunately, Pearce was to confirm this general tendency as his last significant contribution to our knowledge of ESP. After more than two years of brilliant work, in which he mastered difficulty after difficulty and carried through one project after another, the thing I had been dreading happened.

How Pearce came to lose his capacity for exceptional extra-sensory work is a personal story: One morning he received a letter which greatly distressed him. Before coming to our laboratory he mentioned this letter and its effect upon him to five different people, including myself, and actually showed the letter to one member of the laboratory group, giving some additional personal details to explain his reaction to it. Pearce openly declared that he doubted his ability to do any effective work that particular day, because, he said, of the state of mind into which the letter had thrown him.

From then on, Pearce's work has been on a conspicuously different basis. There have been minute flashes of ESP ability, but none at the level of his earlier and more reliable performance. It now seemed to be easier for him to go below chance, if anything, than above it. In the thousands of trials made with him afterward—many of them under the same conditions as those of his previous work— his scores have averaged little better than what could be expected from chance alone. We could not explain this complete and sudden change in his work, though we would have given much to know what happened in his mind. Like our other subjects, he did not know in what way the extra-sensory impressions came to him in the first place, and having lost his confidence he does not know how to return to his old way of perceiving them. In the years since he left Duke he has made occasional attempts to find out whether he could again equal his earlier scoring, but so far he has been unable to do so.

4

Needless to say, the investigation of Pearce occupied the center of the stage for a long time. But there was room for attention to more than one subject, and soon there were plenty of them. Indeed, we had our hands full with more subjects than we could do justice to. Had Pearce not been among us and played the part he did, it is likely that some of the others would have come forward and taken a larger part in the experiments. Likewise, had we been free to give more time to the research, the work of the others would have developed further. The three assistants I had by this time—C. E. Stuart, J. G. Pratt, Sara Ownbey—were all graduate students engaged in pursuing their advanced degrees, and I myself was supposed to be giving full time to other university duties. Without the help of these assistants at that period only a relatively small part of the actual results would have been accomplished.

During the years 1932 and 1933 good subjects

seemed fairly to crowd in upon us. There was Miss June Bailey, who was one of my students and who already had a firm belief that she was capable of unusual and extra-sensory insights. She believed also that some of her relatives were likewise gifted. Her laboratory performances certainly bore out her confidence in her ability. Through some thousands of trials she averaged between 8 and 10 hits on each run.

T. Coleman Cooper, too, had preconceived beliefs regarding his powers, and again there was a family history of such abilities. This was unknown to me when he came into my office one day to consult me on behalf of a friend. Like nearly every other visitor, he was shown the card tests, and he and a companion were persuaded to try calling them. They became deeply interested, and Cooper did remarkably well. Ultimately he was able to score reliably around 8 hits per 25 over thousands of trials. Yet he did as well in my office that first day as he ever did later on.

Another more or less casual contact brought in Miss May Frances Turner, also a student. I believe Miss Turner also came to see me in behalf of one of her friends whom she thought I might be able to help. She, too, belonged to that large number of people who believe that they possess gifts in extra-sensory awareness of things. However, like all those who came into our tests, she was normal and sane

about the whole matter. Her averages through
many thousands of trials were in the neighborhood
of 9. This subject, a quiet and unassuming young
woman, turned out one of the most phenomenal
series on record when the experiments were developed to the point at which the condition of distance was introduced. The story, however, can
wait for a later chapter.

In connection with each of these subjects there
are some interesting personal details. Miss Bailey,
Miss Turner, and Mr. Cooper, for instance, believed that they had more than the ordinary amount
of intuition about people. They took their work
seriously and devotedly, two of them to the extent
that they felt it would be improper to accept the
regular wages. They all had a certain amount of
artistic interest or ability, two of them outstand-
ingly so. All three happened to be Southerners.

There was something of a missionary spirit in our
subjects, and on one occasion when Miss Turner
was good-naturedly challenged by one of her teachers as to the genuineness of her ability she accepted
the challenge and offered to prove it. To her next
class period she brought a pack of cards and gave
them to the instructor, who held them behind a
book while they were being called. She averaged
over 8 hits per 25 in the four runs that were made.
This was significant scoring in itself; it would not
happen by chance alone once in 150 such series.

Very few subjects probably could have performed under such conditions; they would hardly have had the confidence and courage.

Oddest of all is the way we came to discover that Miss Sara Ownbey was a good ESP subject. Miss Ownbey was a graduate student in psychology who was ably conducting, under my direction, an investigation into hypnotic treatment of a certain physiological derangement of function. One day she happened to witness an informal demonstration of Pearce at work on the ESP tests. Now, Miss Ownbey was a most conscientious person and a devoted friend. She came to me and out of the kindness of her heart endeavored to persuade me that there *must* be something wrong, that Pearce must be deceiving me. She thought that in some way or other he was managing to follow cues on the cards. I reviewed some of the precautions we had already taken, such as not allowing subjects an opportunity to mark the cards, using new decks without telling the subject, watching every move the subject made while he was in the laboratory, and using screens behind which the cards were wholly hidden. I tried to show her that deception was impossible so far as we could humanly judge. But she felt sure that something of the sort must be going on, so finally I suggested that she herself take a deck of ESP cards away with her and try calling through a few runs; if she could work out by cues a way of scoring as high as Pearce had done and demonstrate her method under the same laboratory conditions, that demonstration would establish her point better than any argument could.

A few days later she came in blushing, and said, "Oh, Dr. Rhine, I feel so embarrassed!" When I inquired why, she admitted that she had tried some of the card calling and that without needing to employ the "cues" she had been so convinced Pearce was using, she had got, among other scores, one as high as 15.

"Are you satisfied *you* weren't cheating?" I asked her. Indeed she was. She became one of our best subjects, although, because of her pronounced self-consciousness, she was easily disturbed by observation. Her averages ranged between 8 and 11 under different conditions. Though little of her work could be done under my own observation, most of it was supervised by other experimenters whose ability and good faith I do not doubt.

Miss Ownbey, having become interested in the work in extra-sensory perception, became my most active and, on the whole, most gifted assistant. She had an extraordinary ability to keep her subjects in good working humor and at the same time maintain conditions as desired. Never, from the beginning, did she relax her suspicion, and from time to time she would discuss frankly with me the possibility of deception, even by her friends, simply in the interests of scientific caution. For this protective and loyal attitude, as well as for the enormous amount of work done, I acknowledge here the great contribution she rendered this study.

One of our good subjects we owe to a departmental romance. This was another graduate student in the department of psychology, George Zirkle. He and Miss Ownbey had become unusually good friends, and it was natural that she should try out Zirkle's capacities for extra-sensory perception. She was astonished by his scores. As a matter of fact, we all were, including Zirkle himself, although he admitted that occurrences of a psychic nature had happened more than once in his family.

The results of Zirkle's tests were very good. While his average for the entire period of work was between 8 and 9, some of his work ran to almost twice that figure, and on one occasion he equaled Pearce's most sensational run—a perfect score of 25 successive hits. Had Zirkle been in Pearce's place he probably would have done as well. Zirkle worked almost entirely under the direction of Miss Ownbey, which may help to account for the fact that she is now Mrs. Zirkle. Other witnesses were brought in later to observe his tests, and consequently responsibility for the soundness of his work does not rest upon the observation of only one person.

Once, during the period of Zirkle's best work when he was averaging in the neighborhood of 14, he suffered an attack of influenza. It was not severe, but dragged on for approximately two weeks. During this period his scores, though still averaging above 8, represented a great drop from his previous record. After the period of illness was over, his scores again rose to their original level.

In fact, most of our subjects of this period either underwent declines in scoring rate or else stopped taking the tests. Miss Turner, Miss Bailey, and Cooper, for one reason or another, discontinued. The ways in which Linzmayer, Stuart, and Pearce lost their faculty of high scoring have already been described. Both Mr. and Mrs. Zirkle fell off in their scoring abilities about the time of their marriage, though I do not think this happy event had anything to do with the decline unless the very natural shift of interest was a factor. It seems more likely that they, too, had worn out the original interest, and that the kind of interest which remained was of the technical scientific sort, too abstract and intellectual to vitalize an otherwise laborious and monotonous procedure. It is not difficult to appreciate the possibility of getting tired of our tests after being through tens of thousands of them day after day in the same routine way.

At this time we discovered many good subjects of whom there is not space in this book to speak; at least ten others satisfied the statistical requirements for demonstrating some principle beyond chance causation as the explanation of their scores.

The group of 18 of which I speak was selected from a total of about 80 persons whom we tested in our search for subjects. This does not mean that the remaining number had no ESP ability. Few, if any, of them were tested far enough to establish a negative conclusion. None of the subjects tested adequately in our laboratory was completely negative. Two of them reported negative results after what seemed a sufficient number of tests (not made for our records) in their own rooms. There may have been others tested under similar conditions of whom I did not hear. Some of the rest merely yielded initial low results, and since we had many promising subjects, they were not urged to continue. A number did not have sufficient interest to return for further work after a preliminary test period which was not conclusive one way or the other.

However, by this time it seemed entirely safe to estimate that at least one in five of the persons tested showed ESP capacity. It is interesting that in such surveys of the frequency of occurrence of spontaneous psychic experiences as those made by the English Society for Psychical Research and by Dr. Prince of the Boston Society for Psychic Research, the estimates varied from 1 in 4 to 1 in 7 people. Our estimate of 1 in 5 extra-sensorily perceptive persons shows an interesting correlation to these figures.

5

Several questions have been frequently raised concerning what conditions favor discovery of good ESP subjects, especially among those already interested in the phenomena of this field. How did you discover them? What did you do at Duke to get so many subjects? Is it a matter of climate? Is it the southern stock? Is it your personality? Is it the nature of your tests? It is a difficult task to answer these questions adequately, but it is not impossible. The many investigators in other places who have already followed our directions have generally been successful. A few have tried to repeat our tests without following our methods and without keeping in touch with us, and most of these have failed. In one case an experimenter reversed his earlier tactics, began asking us for suggestions, and promptly found some success.

In general little can be said about finding subjects for extra-sensory perception work that cannot equally be said of such well-established human activities as teaching the arts, or any profession requiring particular ability in getting co-operation from other people. I will not attempt here to defend or justify these instructions. So far they have proved effective with us, but it may well be that some of them will later be found less necessary than we believe them to be at present.

First, the investigator himself should be interested in obtaining good results—high scores. If for any reason he is not, he should be able to lay aside his inhibitions and play his part as a good sport. A critical or fussy investigator would be as much out of place in this kind of work as he would be as cheerleader at a football game or as teacher in a school.

The better the investigator can communicate a wholehearted enthusiasm, confidence, and encouragement to the subjects, the better are his chances for success. Some subjects require a challenging attitude, others a sympathetic one. Some will need to have their attention kept from resting too much on the scores and technicalities of their work, others ought to be taken fully into the confidence of the investigator.

The experimenter must maintain a high level of interest on the part of the subject throughout the experiment. But it is important to emphasize that this interest must not be a merely intellectual one. For that reason complicated intellectual discussions and arguments are best left out of the laboratory. The subject should be made as curious and eager as possible to see what scores he can make. If the subject cannot maintain curiosity and interest of an active character, it is better to discontinue the tests.

I attribute my own difficulties as a subject to this overdeveloped intellectual interest in the process.

When I begin taking the tests I soon become furiously introspective and want to know what is taking place in my own mind. I wonder about my score, and many of the daily associations of the research come crowding into consciousness. Then I am lost so far as extra-sensory perception is concerned. Only when I catch myself off guard can I keep above chance average. By calling 5, 10, or at most 15 cards, and stopping when my intruding ulterior interests are aroused, I can score at the average of 7 hits per 25. My first 215 calls averaged but slightly under this and are significant. But in a later series of 1,650 calls made with no regard for mental state I averaged only 5.3 hits per 25, which is too slightly above chance to be reliable.

I have often felt that experience as a salesman in my college days has stood me in good stead in directing this research. The task of the salesman, in the best sense of that word, is to inspire interest and enthusiasm and create confidence. For some people this is by training or native ability a difficult thing to do, while for others it is easy. Those who find it hard should not undertake to experiment in this field, just as, I think it would be agreed, they should not undertake to carry out experiments in hypnotic research or in any other work in which suggestion or the direct personal influence on the actions of others is an essential to success. It is interesting to observe that a number of those who have been successful in this work have also been

successful hypnotists. Professor Richet, Dr. Estabrooks, some of my assistants here, such as Mrs.
Zirkle (Miss Ownbey), Dr. Pratt, Mr. Stuart, and
myself, not to mention a number of Continental
physicians such as Dr. Alfred Backman, of Sweden,
Pierre Janet, of France, and several others who figure in the literature of the subject.

However difficult it may be to help subjects to
score well in ESP tests, it is easy enough to prevent
their doing so. I have already described a number of
the conditions which will do this, but I shall repeat
them here. First, if there is a strongly distracting
situation, such as the presence of a number of
witnesses or being "put on the spot," failure is assured. If the subject is placed in a critical atmosphere and made to feel that the task is a hopeless
one, he is pretty certain to fail. If he is not interested
or is antagonistic to the research or the investigator,
a negative deviation instead of a positive one may
result. Certainly a positive one cannot be expected.
Narcotic drugs, of course, lower scores, but even
the mildly narcotic effect of extreme fatigue or
sleepiness is enough to lessen the likelihood of good
results, as indeed is the case in other sorts of work.

The thing that is most likely to prevent good
scoring in psychological laboratories is a wooden
and inflexible routine into which the subject has to
fit himself no matter how he is feeling and regardless of his degree of interest—a routine to which
he must adhere until his daily requirement of tests

is fulfilled. At Duke we tried testing forty subjects under such a cut-and-dried system and found only one good scorer in the lot. On the other hand, by picking up whoever comes along, and using as much tact and salesmanship (if you like) as we can, we succeed much more often than not in getting a significant score once friendly co-operation is fully established.

CHAPTER VII

The First Serious Criticism

AT THIS STAGE OF THE STORY NOBODY SHOULD take the existence of extra-sensory perception on faith. What the two preceding chapters have done is to describe certain experiments with cards, tell about the scores which some subjects were able to make with them, and quote the odds against guesswork or chance as the explanation. The tests as a whole, or in their natural subdivisions, gave results that are clearly beyond the best that could be expected from the so-called laws of luck. A figure of over a thousand digits would be required to express the unlikelihood of that solution. Some other factor was causing our results, and so far it has been called "extra-sensory perception" in a noncommittal way.

In explaining the results of these tests a mere abstract citation of mathematical odds against chance as the explanation of our findings is not sufficient. People want every question and doubt answered before they are convinced, and indeed it is sensible to look over again and again every possible alternative before accepting such a revolutionary explanation as our hypothesis of extra-sensory perception. Then, too, the tests on which it is based are so incompatible with certain widely ac-

cepted points of view that even though we have
found many subjects who can produce high scores
there is perhaps a flaw in the method itself or in the
way of handling the results. *Is chance really excluded by the mathematics used?* However conclusive the figures appear, is there not a possibility that
the mathematics used in deriving them is faulty or
is wrongly applied?

Now, of course, my associates—particularly Mr.
Stuart, who is mathematically trained—and I have
been asking ourselves these questions from the very
beginning. We have had others doing it in other
places. We have been in touch with mathematical
people all along the way, but most readers have not.
For their sake I shall take up these questions here
and see if I can show whether we have adequately
excluded chance as a possible explanation. This is
important because, if there is doubt at this crucial
point, the rest of this book will not be even interesting.

2

To begin with, let us take a simple, common-
sense view of the results of the tests. On that basis
there are two things to be compared: (1) the scores
a subject gets by actually calling the cards through
a long series of runs and (2) the scores secured in
tests where no subjects called the cards at all—
simply cross-matching one deck against another. As
we have already seen, thousands of these tests have

worked out to an average of almost exactly 5.0, and when you reflect that mechanical shufflers have been employed in some of these control tests, as they are called, it is impossible to believe that they did not exclude the faculty or condition, or whatever it was, that made the higher scores of the human subjects possible. But that is not all the precaution we have taken on this point. Thousands and thousands of other matchings have been made to cross-check calls by the subjects themselves. This is easily done by using a different pack from the one against which he made his calls—say, the order of the deck in the *run before* or the *run after*. Thus, the records of the subject's calls in his second run are compared with the actual order of the cards in his first or his third run. This, too, ought to exclude extra-sensory perception because the calls were never intended for the cards against which they are checked.

One of the very first things that was done in the evaluation of Pearce's scoring was to take his first thousand ESP trials and compare them with a thousand card records taken from the same pack of cards when no extra-sensory perception was involved. In other words, a thousand of his calls were checked against cards that he did not intend them to match. The cross-check series of 1,000 approximated 5 very closely, giving 5.1 as a result, while Pearce's first thousand trials averaged 9.6 hits per 25, almost double the amount. Various other kinds of cross-checks have been made, as well as the simple

matching of one pack of cards against another, and
in *no case* has there been any important departure
from the theoretical chance average of 5.0. It is
just as easy, then, for one to judge by common sense
that *something* is shown where the results average
9.6 as it would be to look into one's account book
and find that there was a profit if the average sale
amounted to $9.60 and the cost was $5.10.

For a long time one of my friends, who did not
understand the mathematics of probability very
well, kept repeating, "But sometime you may find
your subjects going just as far in the other direction
as now they are going above chance."

In reply I used to appeal to his common sense
and say, "For two years now Pearce, to say nothing
of the others, has been coming in here several days
a week and has been leaving every day a positive
deviation. He *never* goes below chance unless we
ask him to. When we do ask him to go below chance
and deliberately try to miss the cards, he can do
so, sometimes scoring zero. The fact that he can go
low at will and can regularly go high for so long
a period must be the answer to your claim that we
are having just a run of luck. Such voluntary scoring is the very opposite of chance. This man can
get a score of 9 or 10 if I ask him for a high score;
if I ask him to run low, he can get a 1 or 0; can
go back up on the next run if I say 'high' and down
on the run succeeding that if I say 'low.' If this is
a matter of chance performance, then the rise and

fall of that steam shovel I see out the window is a chance performance. And even if the subject does reverse later, and go regularly below for two years? A man may make money on his sales every day for two years; then he may turn round and sell at a loss for the next two years and lose it all again. Is that to say that the whole performance was merely chance?"

3

Most striking to the people who want the point made as simple as possible are the long unbroken stretches of successive hits. Even 5 successive hits represents odds of more than 3,000 to 1 against a chance occurrence. But when one gets up into 9's, 15's, and finally 25's, one need only know the multiplication table to follow through and find out what the chances are of such an event's being due to nothing but random factors. Or you can even dispense with the multiplication table. Actually, all we have to convince us of the occurrence of things in life is simple repetition in unbroken succession. Apply the simple, everyday rules of common sense to these long stretches, and few people would be likely to say they were accidental.

Fortunately for the skeptics of common sense, the mathematics which applies to these cases has been in use for many years and has been recognized over and over again by the authorities in the field of special determinations of probability. It was first applied to these problems back in the eighties and nineties by the physiologist, Professor Richet, and it was then used essentially as today. It was used again by Coover (who, you will recall, mistook his evidence to be against nonsensory perception), by Estabrooks, and by several others, including the experts called in to evaluate the results of the widely publicized *Scientific American* tests for telepathy. It has had the endorsement of the leading authorities of England and America. To my knowledge no question of its validity has been raised by any professional statistician or mathematician of probability.

Granted, then, that the mathematics is sound and appropriate to these results, have we somehow made a mistake in the way we have applied it? There is a good test for this too: we may know reliably that we have not made such a mistake, because we get only figures appropriate to chance when we apply the mathematical tests in the same way to experiments carried out under conditions identical in every point with the test experiments, except that, since no human mind has made any of the calls in the series, ESP has been so positively excluded that only chance factors can possibly be operative. From these non-ESP experiments we get the same results to be anticipated from mere chance data. At the moment of writing, a group of papers is going to press for the *Journal of Parapsychology* reporting such parallel experiments. In every case chance conditions give figures that would be expected. In every case the ESP tests, differing only in that extra-sensory perception was allowed to operate if it could, show that something beyond chance is at work. There is logically no criticism left to level at the use of the mathematics in the case.

So much for chance. We have had it as our ever-present competitor. We have always been alert to its claims. But as a theory for these results it "hasn't a chance"!

But suppose the subject has personal preferences and calls twice as many circles as other symbols. Might this not favor him? The answer is "no" since, even if he called all 25 of the cards circles, the most he could get would be 5. The more circles he calls the greater chance he has, of course, of getting a good proportionate score among the five circles in the pack, but a proportionately small chance is left for his getting the other twenty cards right. Preference cannot help him on his total score.

Can any method of shuffling the cards or any natural sequence of cuts give peculiar upcurves or downcurves in the scoring of these control series? The many practical test checks that have been made on just this point furnish the best answer. They average close to 5, with no long-drawn-out stretches of runs that would yield significant deviations.

For years one of the most common objections that we encountered was: "But might not the subject use reasoning, as in card games? Suppose he has called all the symbols five times over except one—let us say, star—and he has two calls to make. Will he not reason that these now must be stars because he has called all the others?" Obviously, as I have suggested already, he has no way of knowing whether or not the other calls have been correct, so it would be most unfounded reasoning to conclude that the last two must be stars. Only if he knew the correctness of the cards already called could reasoning help him, and this he does not know. Therefore, the chances remain the same on the twenty-fifth call as on the first, since he is just as ignorant about what that card is.

"Might not a subject use some system of advantage to him?" How can he, if he has nothing to go on? If he does not know whether his calls are correct or incorrect, no system could work. A system without a basis in fact would be nothing but a delusion.

A curious question has been raised and vehemently urged in one or two places. It is supposed that all our investigators in this research might be stopping at some strategic moment — say, after some high scores have been made and just before a series of low ones might be made. The very essence of this question is to assume that we can tell somehow by previous runs what the next ones are going to be. If our results are due to chance, this could not be done. What we mean by the term "chance" is the very absence of a fixed order and predictability. However, to settle the matter, one of my critical colleagues, who believed this was a weakness in our work, tested out the supposed principle in actual experimentation and found no evidence of it.

At times we have been told that perhaps something is wrong with our using a pack of 25 cards, and we have been urged to try packs of 100 or 1,000. There are no adequate mathematical grounds available for such insistence, and even from a common-sense point of view it is difficult to see what difference it would make. However, some of our best work has been done without adhering strictly to a pack of 25. It will be recalled that Pearce's twenty-five straight successes were made by calling one card, checking it at once, returning it to the pack, and cutting. In this way the pack was an unending one. It might have been a hundred or a thousand or any other number. Considerable later work has been done with packs of 50, and on some occasions of even larger size.

4

After weighing all the criticism we have been able to get in seven years' time, I have come to feel as much security in the general soundness of the research as is good for an investigator in science to have. Reflecting upon the enormous amount of work that has been done here and elsewhere, it seems

A SHUFFLING BOX TO INSURE MECHANICAL SHUFFLING.
THE LID IS PUT ON AND THE BOX SLOWLY TIPPED, ONE
END UP AND THEN DOWN, NOT LESS THAN FIVE TIMES.
FIVE ESP CARDS ARE DISPLAYED AGAINST THE LID OF
THE BOX.

to me that no inferential scientific conclusion has ever had so much evidence in its support; that is, in excluding a chance hypothesis. The mathematics *has* been questioned, yes, but not by a single mathematician. Two psychologists have written a total of four articles criticizing it, but the author of three of them has become satisfied that his criticisms do no apply now that he has what he feels is sufficient further information. A third psychologist has more recently published a review of the criticisms, and he asserts that the statistics used in this research are substantially correct.

Among mathematicians the best authority is with us. Confirmatory mathematical checks have mounted by tens of thousands, not only in this laboratory but in a number of other places. It is difficult to see what further mathematical criteria can be applied to evaluate the results of our tests.

Thus far, it would appear, we have been on sound territory. Whatever we have claimed to be beyond chance has stood the tests and is safe. But our experiments are still going on. They are going on into yet more meaningful, more revolutionary lines. The strain upon this mathematics of probability will be increasingly great with every advancing step along the lines we are at present following. With the enormously greater burden anticipated for this technique of evaluation, it is high time that we secure the last word, both in criticism and in support. We shall need it.

CHAPTER VIII

Is It Sensory or Extra-Sensory?

IF THE RESULTS IN OUR EXPERIMENTATION CAN-
not be explained by chance, what is the next weak-
est link to be inspected? Most critical people would
suggest that the accurate calls might be actually
due to sensory rather than extra-sensory cues; that
is, some kind of signal to the subject who is calling
the cards. Several such almost-imperceptible indications, conveyed by one of the recognized senses,
are conceivable. In the third chapter we mentioned
that the psychologist Lehmann thought the early
results of the English Society for Psychical Research
were due to involuntary whispering, which, of
course, would give auditory sensory cues.

In this card work, however, since no one knew
what symbol a given card contained, it would be
necessary to look for visual sensory cues or tactual
ones obtained from touching the cards. Such cues
might be quite unconsciously perceived by the
subject, as psychologists know, though such unconscious perception would be rather unusual. Furthermore, we have to allow for the possibility of especially sensitive vision or touch, something beyond
that of the average individual. A few people may

even suppose that our good subjects are simply individuals with unusually acute sensory or tactual sensation, technically called "hyperesthesia."
Whether or not any great amount of hyperesthesia
ever actually occurs is doubtful, but to some people
almost anything is more reasonable than the conclusion that extra-sensory perception is a fact.

The best way of answering the question, "Will
sensory cues explain the Duke results?" is to judge
for yourself from a brief account of the results. Let
us begin with the simplest argument against the
occurrence of sensory cues: If there are sensory cues
on the cards themselves, then there must be, of
course, marks or peculiarities on them. Second, these
marks must be in some way linked up by the subject with the symbols on the faces of the cards.
He will have to know the connection between the
marks and the symbols, and that in turn presupposes
an opportunity to learn this connection. Otherwise
the supposed marks will simply not work as sensory cues for him. The easiest way to avoid this
possibility is to use new cards which have never been
in his hands before.

Pass over the fact that with the hundreds of packs
of cards that have been used in the laboratory there
must always have been first runs which would
not have allowed the subject an opportunity to
acquire sensory cues. Ignore the point that it is
extremely difficult for anyone to learn such cues
when he can see only the backs of the cards at the

time he is calling twenty-five in succession, and their faces only when the cards are turned over at the checkup. Finally, overlook the further point that some subjects, of whom Zirkle is a conspicuous example, never glance at the cards at all when they are calling them, and others, like Miss Bailey and Pearce, look at the cards only rarely. Omitting all these considerations, let me cite a definite and precise experiment designed to meet this point. I took twenty-five new packs of cards and gave them out one at a time to Pearce, who was at this time being allowed to handle the cards himself. I did not call any special attention to the cards' being new. He was given three runs each with these new decks in the usual way. Now, if sensory cues were being followed, the results of the first runs with each of these new packs placed before Pearce for the first time should have dropped to an average of the chance expectation—5.0. Instead, they were well above 9 and were quite on a par with the results of his work on other packs at that time. The second and third runs were very close also: they averaged, for all the decks, 9.4, 9.2, and 9.8.

When investigators into extra-sensory phenomena claim to achieve results as startling as ours, certain people believe that they can be explained away by a particular type of expert. Perhaps because of the work of the late Harry Houdini, magicians are quite widely believed to be able to duplicate almost any phenomenon that is hard for the rest of us to explain. On one occasion when I was working with Pearce I invited my friend Wallace Lee, the well-known magician, to watch Pearce's tests. Not only did Lee generously admit that he saw no way in which Pearce might be employing sensory cues, but when invited to do so, he tried to duplicate Pearce's results under identical conditions and without success. He told us frankly that he was convinced of the absence of any kind of useful sensory indication on the cards and confessed that Pearce's scores mystified him. Naturally Lee is familiar with a wide range of forms of deception based on sensory cues, and the story of his visit may therefore interest those people who feel that sensory cues (or trickery) can possibly explain our results.

2

So far, then, as sensory cues on the cards themselves are concerned, these answers are probably all that even the severest critic could demand.

But is it possible that the card face was reflected from some shiny surface? No, for in most tests the card was called *before* it was lifted from the pack. The particular technique for this kind of test is called "BT"—before touching. It means simply that each card is called before it is touched by anyone.

There is no better way of answering questions in this field, however, than by answering them in ten different experimental ways. Therefore, suppose that there is something inadequate about the check results furnished by working with new packs. The DT work must then be considered next. DT means "down through," calling the cards down through the pack without removing any of them until the whole pack has been called. Thus the subject is able to see the back of only the top card, and even if there had been a code mark actually *printed* or otherwise indicated on the back of each card, and the subject had memorized the code of marks, he would still have been unable to get sensory help on any but the top card. At first some subjects felt that DT was a much more difficult procedure and hesitated to try it, but eventually most of them did it successfully. Although they did not seem to do it as successfully as when the BT technique was employed, the difficulty was evidently psychological, as was proved by an analysis of the results. More hits were made in the first five calls and in the last five calls down through the pack than were made in the fifteen cards between. There seemed to be some difficulty in keeping track of the cards through the center of the pack, which again suggests more familiar mental processes like memorizing. For instance, Pearce averaged about 7.5 on his DT work; this score is a significant one, and high enough to prove the point that he could not have been depending upon sensory cues.

Another way of testing for sensory cues was the

simple one of placing an opaque screen in front of
the cards so that the subject could not see them. In
the screen trials with Pearce, his averages for different conditions ran between 8.3 and 9.7. In other
words, the elimination of the possibility of sensory
cues by using a screen did not retard his good scoring. With our present work in the laboratory, the
screening has become almost a routine condition.
Many of the results of the more recent work with
newly developed types of screens has already been
printed in the *Journal of Parapsychology*. At
Tarkio College (Tarkio, Missouri), J. L. Woodruff
and Dr. R. W. George found a man who did much
better scoring with a screen than without it. Perhaps the climax in screening thus far has been
reached in the experiments at Duke of the Misses
Margaret M. Price and Margaret H. Pegram, who
screened the cards even when working with blind-
from-birth subjects, and still obtained scores indicating extra-sensory perception. In one series of
tests the cards, in addition to being screened, were
sealed in opaque envelopes, but this did not prevent
the blind subjects from perceiving the symbols inside.

Later in this book there will be an account of a
dramatic series of tests that still further bears out
our contention that sensory cues are not the answer
to the high scores made by our subjects. These are
the runs made when the subject and the investigator
were separated by distance, in some cases as much

as a 100 yards, and actually situated in different buildings. Scores made under these conditions were more than significant, and sensory cues were playing no part in producing them. In later publications, too, there will be more of these distance tests with even greater distances.

3

But even if none of the known senses can account for the results of these ESP tests, what about the "sixth sense"? May we not have evidence here of a hidden, an unknown sense? The natural tendency upon examining our results is to conclude offhand that we are dealing with an unknown sense. When Frederic Myers invented the word "telesthesia" to cover what we are calling "clairvoyance" in this book, he apparently intended the term to mean literally "sensing at a distance." For a similar purpose Professor Richet coined the word "cryptesthesia," which means "hidden sense." Other such terms have been devised.

The trouble with this idea of a new "sixth" sense is that the extra-sensory perceptive phenomenon does not behave like sensation. All we know about it so far fails to agree with any version of the sensory theory—call it "hidden," "cryptic," "sixth," or what you will. In ESP there is no *experience of localization* as there is with the senses; no one can say as yet that any particular part of the body receives the ESP impression. Some subjects think they can, but this idea is easily proved an hallucination. What is more, no angle of orientation is needed. A subject may turn any part of his body toward the card with equal success.

With the most comparable sense—vision—the angle of the card is important too. Not so with extra-sensory perception. Distance from the object also is enormously important to the senses. Apparently not to ESP. Big symbols are more easily seen than very small ones, but in ESP either an enormously wide range of perception is possible or else it makes no reliable difference how large or small the symbol is. Mrs. Rhine has thoroughly demonstrated this fact in work with child subjects, and the few similar tests with Pearce, which I mentioned earlier, had indicated this to be true. It is possible, of course, that none of these tests is exhaustive enough to be final on the distinction between sensory and extra-sensory perception. But from the survey of the facts now at hand it appears that extra-sensory perception is fundamentally different from sensation. Certainly in ESP no known energy serves as the medium to convey the impression to the percipient. All the common ones have been ruled out, as we shall see later on.

Many other processes of the mind are not sensory either. Reasoning, memory, and all the imaginational judgments which men use in creative work, whether it be artistic, religious, or some other kind,

130 NEW FRONTIERS OF THE MIND

are also made in the absence of objective sensory stimuli. They are, of course, perceptual, they do not furnish direct knowledge of the outside world, and their processes are just as far beyond the senses as is this unknown mode of perception which we are investigating; it does not supernaturalize the mind simply to discover that it has some extra-sensory capacities in the field of perception. No discriminating person, therefore, will view our findings as mystical, occult, or supernatural merely because they are not based on sensory reports.

Some of the people who have taken an interest in these experiments have suggested the hypothesis that extra-sensory perception is due to a primordial sense, now atavistic in man; that it came before the other senses, is more general, and perhaps depends on every body cell for its reception. Others consider it a superdevelopment of the five senses, a crowning achievement of the nervous system, and the frail signs of it that we find are but the promise of great powers toward which we are evolving.

But until there is forthcoming some better evidence favoring the view that what we call ESP is sensory, or is like the senses in at least some respects, I cannot see any encouragement for either of these views. I am more inclined to expect the final explanation to come from a fundamental readjustment of our view of mind and its relation to the world of the senses. For several centuries we have been trying to fit mind into the materialistic world of sensation. If it does not wholly fit in, perhaps this is because it has properties which are just as reliable and lawful, but different. There is nothing unscientific about this. The idea appears to me to be fully naturalistic. On the other hand, I hope to avoid blinding myself to any of the facts because of the extreme antimystical terror to which many scientists are subject. It is dangerous to be stampeded in either direction on this most significant issue.

4

A few persons may be willing to believe that every one of the investigators in the Duke experiments has been so incompetent all these years as persistently to make errors in the same direction, thus accounting for the high scores reported. Actually one English critic went so far as to write us that for him this explanation was preferable to the theory of clairvoyance. He could accept telepathy; but clairvoyance? Rather the theory of cumulative error! No matter if several persons are involved, they must all be making errors repeatedly in the same direction. The only way I can answer this critic is to refer him to the next chapter, which describes the discoveries made by investigators in colleges and universities outside Duke. If other researches keep on substantiating ours, he will eventually give up his belief that we are poor calculators or scorers.

I know, too, that there is at least one critic, also an Englishman, who believes that my assistants, subjects, and colleagues have all been "pulling my leg," practicing a systematic and consummate deception. Such an event would not be entirely without precedent. There is a rumor about a chemist who was seeking to transmute mercury into gold and who had an assistant more sympathetic than reliable. This assistant dropped traces of gold into the solution in order to encourage his chief, presumably believing that the gold ought theoretically to be there anyhow! A great Russian scientist is supposed to have been victimized by a too-helpful assistant who anticipated the outcome of the experiment and helped it along in the wrong way. Best known of all is the German geologist whose students prankishly buried fossils for him to "discover," arranged in line with his own theory, finally even helping him to dig up one bearing his own initials.

I could put up a strong defense, I believe, for the generally fine character of the group of men and women with whom I have worked. The "leg-pulling" conspiracy would have to include members of my own family and persons who are now staff members of college institutions; in all, a score of persons, some of whom did not know one another. But again the easiest reply is reference to the findings of researches in other places.

Of all the obstacles to acceptance of the evidence for ESP, the most difficult to deal with is that which the critic cannot himself formulate. "There must be a snag in it somewhere," he will say. "You have not given enough details" is another way of saying that he cannot see what is wrong but is quite sure that something is.

Recently a distinguished chemist visited our laboratory and generously spent several hours arguing that there must be something basically wrong with our work—purely on general grounds. He had several times helped to expose error in his own field and felt that he knew the erroneous type of work by its general appearance, by certain symptoms. He did not see the particular snag in our case, but he knew it was there! He will, however, find it much harder to suppose an invisible snag in a dozen different researches, conducted with different conditions and personnel, than in the case of a solitary project.

In science it is customary to suspend judgment on a new discovery until it is confirmed by another laboratory. Rarely is more than one such repetition needed unless there is special reason for being doubtful. If the Duke research had remained unconfirmed for a long time, its standing would have been a relatively insecure one. Fortunately, it did not stand alone even at the start. As the third chapter has already made clear, it followed a long series of investigations of extra-sensory perception. And in turn it has been followed by a long series of researches of still better quality, on the whole, than those which preceded it.

CHAPTER IX

The Work of Other Laboratories

ONE OF THE MOST INTERESTING INVESTIGATIONS of extra-sensory phenomena conducted by research workers in outside laboratories was begun even before the first results of the Duke experiments were published in 1934. It was, therefore, an entirely independent study. The experimenter, Dr. Hans Bender, was a young psychologist at the German university of Bonn. In 1933 he began tests which led him to conclude that extra-sensory perception is a genuine occurrence, and which made at least a beginning on the task of finding out where this process fits into the recognized system of mind.

The work consisted of tests for clairvoyance made on a single subject—a graduate student, Fräulein D—at Bonn. Dr. Bender had discovered the capacities of Fräulein D while he was making some explorations into automatic movements and using an ouija board as part of his technique. In the course of these tests he became aware that his subject was responding to letters without looking at them even when she had not seen or otherwise known their positions. In follow-up tests he became convinced that she was clairvoyant. Although this work was done independently of the experiments at Duke, and followed a quite different method, its confirmation of the American findings is clear at many points in Bender's report. And, in addition, it made an original contribution to our knowledge of the field.

In further experiments with Fräulein D, Bender used 27 cards on which were drawn the 26 letters of the alphabet and also a period, or point. These cards were placed in separate opaque envelopes by an assistant and shuffled so that Bender himself did not know, when he chose one, what letter he had. He handed the envelope to the subject, who was in a reclining position, and she held it under a heavy dark cloth. Under this cloth she removed the card from the envelope and handled it freely. The card was covered with heavy cellophane, which eliminated any possible tactual cues. This condition, in which the subject handled the card, was the least guarded one that Bender used. Several other conditions were tried—among them one where the envelope was placed in a box on a shelf, and another in which it was pinned to a curtain behind the seated subject. But under none of these conditions did the subject succeed so well as when having tactual contact with the cellophane-covered card.

Bender himself took a record of all remarks the subject made. In some cases she made drawings as well. These drawings give the impression that in a peculiar, groping way the subject was unquestionably perceiving the letter on the card in more instances than she could have done by chance alone. Bender does not give a statistical treatment of his work and he carried out too few tests; in all, there were only 134. There were 37 successes. If each envelope be counted as a single trial, only 5 successes would be expected by chance alone. A control experiment which was carried out in connection with this work gives the best assurance that more than mere chance was operative in Bender's experiment. In this control test another envelope was chosen against which to match the subject's responses, simply as a check. From Bender's report it is easy to see without the aid of mathematical treatment that the subject did better on the envelopes she was trying to perceive than on the control series that were simply selected arbitrarily.

Even some of the subject's mistakes are suggestive and illuminating. Something of the form-quality of the letter would show up in these trials more often than not, even if she failed to get the whole letter. For instance, rounded figures would be drawn in cases where the card with which she was working carried a letter such as O, C, or Q, and angular ones for letters like K, T, L.

It was this similarity of the form-quality to the letter on the card that specially interested Bender and led him to make what is a unique contribution to the study. He found that when his subject was trying to get a letter form by extra-sensory perception she got first a vague, fragmentary image which became more and more like the letter involved until at last it was clear enough for recognition. Bender knew that the early, fragmentary bits of a visual image which his subject got when perceiving by ESP were much like the images a subject gets when seeing a similar card imperfectly with normal vision in dim light. In one series he had his subject make two tests on each card. First she tried to determine the symbol on the card by ESP and, incidentally, made drawings of all the various images she got for it. Then for the second test she used an apparatus by which the experimenter could increase the illumination thrown on the letter until it came from total invisibility into a clarity sufficient for its recognition. She made drawings of the first dim images in this case too, and so had a set of drawings from ESP and another from dim vision. There is considerable similarity between the two types of images.

I do not think that Bender concludes that these results give him anything like an understanding of the basic process of extra-sensory perception. He recognizes that he is dealing here only with a secondary aspect: the *result* of the process as it appears in the subject's consciousness as a perceptual judgment or choice. The fundamental process below the conscious level is still beyond reach and is, as he points out, not available to introspection. In other words, the subject is entirely unconscious of the real process she is using, and hence can tell nothing about it by looking within herself and describing what seems to her to be happening. But any advance into the uncharted field of extra-sensory perception is important. Even to know, as Bender's study shows, that there is strong similarity between the way ESP impressions and the first visual ones come to consciousness is a real advance in our knowledge.

2

Perhaps the most unusual and dramatic series of observations on a single individual ever made under academic scientific auspices was that recently reported by Professor Ferdinand Neureiter of the Medical School at Riga. His attention was called to the case of a feeble-minded child who was said to be able to read only when her teacher looked at the words in the book along with her. Professor Neureiter describes a number of tests made by himself and others, assuring themselves that the child in some way, without the use of the recognized senses, made contact with the minds of those about her. This extra-sensory perception of mental states, or telepathy, apparently occurred even when the girl was separated from the sender by being stationed in a different room. Newspaper reports and correspondence, however, indicate that this apparently remarkable though unfortunate child is still the center of a great deal of attention from many inquirers, not all of them fully satisfied about the adequacy of the conditions. Interesting and apparently convincing though Neureiter's report is, the case is too extraordinary and important for more than a suspended judgment at present.

3

Let us turn now to work which has followed on that done here at Duke and which has in some measure been stimulated by it. The first case to reach publication was that of Mr. G. N. M. Tyrrell in England. Tyrrell is not an academic man, but his acquaintance with this research obviously goes back many years, since he made a report of some similar experiments in 1922. His work is carried out in his private laboratory and is reported in the *Proceedings* of the English Society for Psychical Research. The outstanding feature of the Tyrrell work is the emphasis upon "motorizing" the responses of the subject: giving her a chance to respond by movement rather than by thinking of symbols. This is the other extreme from the Bender work, in which concentration was upon visual images.

To permit the subject to respond by simple movement, Tyrrell has progressed through several steps to an elaborate machine driven electrically.

The central part of the apparatus consists of a row of five boxes with lightproof sides and lids. Inside each box is a small electric bulb, but in only one box at a time is the bulb lighted. The task of the subject is to open the box containing the lighted bulb, and the success or failure of her choice is recorded automatically when she lifts a lid. Tyrrell is trying to develop a completely automatic machine covering all points, including the choice of the particular box in which the light is to be turned on. Everything about the testing process is to be mechanical except the response of the subject. Although he has not yet succeeded in perfecting his machine, we must remember that it is very difficult to design a mechanism as intricate as this one.

Perhaps the deepest concern one may rightly have about this machine is that so far it does not leave a record both of the choices made by the subject *and* of the boxes actually lighted. Thus the cross-check of actual records, which is such a great safeguard against certain errors, is not yet possible with it. Again, suspended judgment is probably in order.

At different stages in the development of the machine Tyrrell's subject has been obtaining scores above the level of the chance average. His plan has been, as was ours, to try first to get high scores before changing to more rigid testing conditions— first having the subject demonstrate extra-chance scoring and then advancing the precautions. He has been working almost entirely with one sub-ject, Miss G. M. Johnson, with whom he began his studies back in 1922, and she has in time success-fully overcome the difficulty of each new advance. Tyrrell has, however, some results under his most advanced conditions: mechanical selection of the box to be lighted for the subject's test. This, if ade-quate, would tend to rule out any possibility of the subject's simply falling in line with some pe-culiar habit which the experimenter himself might exhibit when he is doing the selecting of the box.

As a matter of fact, the best assurance of Tyr-rell's having discovered a genuine case of extra-sensory perception may be, after all, the few series of runs he has had Miss Johnson make with ESP cards like those used by our laboratory. In these her work has met his criteria of significance, and this fact, together with his own machine tests, leaves one reasonably confident that his work has a sound basis and a brilliant future. The continued development of his machine may well solve many problems of this field.

4

The most gratifying sequel to the experiments at Duke has been the reaction among other Ameri-can college groups. Within a year after the publica-tion of the first scientific report on our experiments work was started in several institutions, and now, some three years later, at least a score of places have, to my knowledge, undertaken something by way of tests of extra-sensory perception, using the card-calling technique. A dozen of these have rounded out projects which merit publication and confirm the basic principle of the Duke work: that subjects can achieve significant extra-chance scores on various card-calling techniques. So far as I know only three have failed to confirm it, and those are the three series conducted with the least regard for the Duke procedure. They were not done under the direction of anyone with experience in this difficult field. All research workers who have closely co-operated with us thus far, and some who have not consulted with us in any important way, have achieved a measure of positive results, although a few are as yet too indefinite for final decision.

Of the twelve confirmatory instances, a half dozen have already been published. As a group they appear to answer pretty definitely the objection that proof of the existence of extra-sensory perception is confined to the Duke experiments.

The first American confirmation of any proportion was, I think, that of Miss Margaret Pegram of Guilford College, North Carolina. Miss Pegram used only herself for subject in the card-calling tests. Perhaps it is just as well, since I am sure no other human being would have put up with the slavish treatment she dealt herself. In less than a year's time she went through more tests than all of us at Duke put together had given all our subjects over a period of four years. She did approximately 185,000 trials, sometimes as many as 5,000 in one day.

Her scores were not very high. They averaged between 5 and 6, varying from 5.3 to 5.6 hits per 25 trials. But with such a huge number of trials even small margins are important. Miss Pegram's work definitely showed something beyond chance. Not only did she demonstrate this in the usual way, but she reversed her method and called for low scores—tried to miss the symbols—and found that she could obtain better deviations by doing so than when trying to make hits.

Miss Pegram's work was not witnessed, and she did her own recording and checking. But she was an assistant in the psychology department at Guilford College, and what is perhaps more reassuring to the reader, has since done scoring in the presence of witnesses at a higher rate and for series of appreciable length. This confirmatory work was carried on at Duke in our Parapsychology Laboratory. She made one long series of runs while she was at Guilford College in which she attempted to call cards placed at Duke University. The distance is over 60 miles. The results gave approximately the same deviation as those she secured when the cards were before her.

5

At Tarkio College there was an earnest young student of psychology, J. L. Woodruff, who believed in ESP and a skeptical instructor who did not. Although he had heard of the Duke experiments Dr. George had never been convinced by them, but he was broad-minded enough to recognize the importance of testing to find out the truth. Woodruff was another example of a man who had his interest in the possibility of extra-sensory perception aroused by experiences in his own family. He proposed to carry out a project in connection with the course in experimental psychology which he was taking under Dr. George. Out of that challenge grew a successful research project, which lasted through the succeeding year and is still going on at Tarkio College.

Woodruff quickly discovered a number of promising subjects and selected three for further experimentation. One was himself. Working with the ESP cards, which in half the experiments were behind screens and in the other half not, he compared three types of technique.

One of these methods was an interesting development of the matching technique. Ordinarily matching tests are carried on by asking the subject to distribute a pack of cards, all face down, opposite a row of five ESP cards (one each of the five symbols) lying face upward on the table in front of him.

He tries to lay each of the cards of the pack, still face downward, opposite its corresponding key card in the row of five. But Woodruff pushed this matching technique a step further: he asked his subjects to match the pack against a row of five key cards also *face down* and in an order unknown to either investigator or subject. The third method Woodruff used was the old BT method in which the top card is called and then removed.

The theory behind this kind of test is that the open-matching technique and, especially, the BT method involve more thinking about the symbols and hence a more cognitive, or mental, mode of response. Matching the cards against a key row which is face downward (blind matching) appears to involve a more motorized response. As we have just seen, Tyrrell was working in the belief that a subject would score higher if he did not have to think of symbols at all, but the results of Woodruff's work show that his subjects did better on the more conscious tests. On the whole, the work at Tarkio was very successful, and since this first research Dr. George has sponsored other projects of equal value.

Another skeptical psychologist states frankly that he began to repeat our tests with the hope of finding out what might be wrong. This man, Dr. C. R. Carpenter, of Bard College, had the feeling from his formal psychological training—not that all psychologists feel that way—that a certain number of trials ought to be given the subject every day

BLIND-MATCHING TEST: THE 5 KEY CARDS ARE FACE
DOWN, IN UNKNOWN ORDER.

and a nicely rounded-out total required of each subject. In other words, the set of tests ought to be completely routinized. With some misgivings we encouraged him to go ahead. It was worth trying, since the worst that could happen was failure. And there was a chance that one good subject might appear among the large number tested. Perhaps there would be one in forty, as we had found at Duke when we ourselves routinized the tests. And that is just about what did happen—the first forty or more that were tested produced one excellent subject and a fair one. The excellent one must have been almost of the caliber of Pearce. How much he was handicapped by the mechanized routine, if indeed he was, no one can say.

At any rate, Carpenter and his assistants tested this subject through long series, resulting in many thousands of trials, and his scores held up consistently through the various conditions under which he was asked to work, including calling the cards down through the deck, and screened BT; that is, removing the card after calling while the pack is behind a small screen that renders it invisible to the subject. The subject failed finally when he was brought up against screened DT: having no contact with the cards whatever and not having the card removed after calling, the pack being behind the screen all the time. However, Carpenter suggests one possible explanation for failure on this test: the pressure upon the subject of his college examinations. Of course, there is no way of knowing what the actual factor was. It may be that the subject lost confidence, a circumstance which has so often accounted for failures in our own tests. Or that he had simply become satiated with ESP tests.

Later, from another smaller sorting of subjects, Carpenter found another good one and another fair one, making four out of something less than seventy subjects tested.

In the Bard College work about half the tests were made with cards in suits of five different colors instead of the five ESP symbols, and in general the results were the same, though slightly higher than with symbols. Carpenter found, too, that the subjects liked working with the colors somewhat better. He—as well as Dr. Harold R. Phalen, who as mathematician joins him in publishing the findings —is unable to explain away ESP, as he had at first hoped to do. It appears more likely that these men may yet help to *explain* it.

6

One of the most interesting pieces of research in the entire field comes not from a college, but from a grade school in Sarasota, Florida. Miss Esther Bond, teaching a group of retarded children, set to work to see what they could do in tests for general extra-sensory perception. She had cards numbering from 1 to 10; after shuffling the pack of 40, she chose from it at random a number upon which to give her attention, asking approximately twenty pupils present from day to day to put down the number upon which she was concentrating. At first she stood in front of the group, studiously avoiding any kind of variation from test to test during the ten trials given daily. During half the series she stood at the rear of the room. She obtained 29 per cent above chance; that is, the average number of hits per day per pupil was 1.29 for ten trials over the sixteen-day period in which the experiment was conducted. The chance average would be about 1. There was some falling off when she shifted to the rear of the room, but still not to the chance level. The scores of some subjects, in fact, rose when the change was made, and a study of the seating chart of the room made it clear that this was not because of the investigator's proximity.

There appeared to be some surprising internal relations in her results that make the study more interesting than it might appear at first glance. One was the fact that the subjects tended to avoid a number when it was the same number as that of the trial. For instance, if number 5 was the card at which the experimenter was looking during the fifth trial, the subject would not get it right even as often as chance would allow. There was apparently some aversion here, some avoidance response. Also, after a pupil had been out of school he did not do well when he first came back, and Monday proved to be the poorest day of the week. Certain pupils, too, stood out above the rest throughout the tests. Later work by the same experimenter, as well as other studies with the young, does not justify the inference that there might have been some relation between the results and the fact that the children were retarded.

Dr. Lucien Warner, psychologist and author of books on comparative psychology, began his exploration in ESP, again under the stimulation, in part at least, of scientific interest in unexplainable experiences among members of his family. Warner was curious to see whether telepathy played a part it was not intended to play in the psychology laboratory; that it might be a factor all unrecognized in certain experiments in the quantitative measurement of sensation. He had the subject lift and judge weights, discriminating between weights that were nearly alike. He made the difference in weight so small that the subject would at a certain stage make one-fourth as many mistakes as successes. At that point Warner introduced the possibility of telepathy to discover whether it altered the score favorably. He explained to the subject the possibility of telepathy and told him that he, as experimenter, would know which weight was the heavier, thus allowing for the transfer of thought.

By use of a screen and carefully controlled technique, Warner was able, he felt, to avoid giving, indirectly or involuntarily, any sensory cues. There-

fore, significant scores should either indicate telepathy or else show that something was wrong with
the conditions, which he and his assistant, Mrs. Mil-
dred Raible, could not discover. The majority of the
subjects did better with telepathy than without it,
and the hits for all combined were almost significant. Two subjects out of the group of seventeen
did markedly better with the telepathic condition,
sufficiently so to satisfy the statistical requirements
for significance. One or two others were quite
promising. Such results led Warner to issue a warning to psychologists to the effect that the possibility
of telepathy in other psychologic experiments
where it is not wanted will have to be taken seriously. There are, of course, many experiments in
which the experimenter knows beforehand the correct thing for the subject to do. Even if he does not,
and there is any objective basis which the subject
could use through clairvoyant perception, it would
be extremely difficult to rule out this possibility.

Warner contends that, difficult as it may be to
do so in many cases, ESP must be taken into account
and not simply ignored. For the comfort of psychologists who may be worried, I would say that it
is one thing to establish the possibility of ESP as a
supplementary factor when consciously tried by the
subject and experimenter and another to show that
it actually does so operate when it is not sought as
an aid. It is a further problem, then, to find out
whether the subject unconsciously uses telepathy

when he is not aware of the possibility of using it. The mere fact that in Warner's control series the subject could have used clairvoyance, but presumably did not do so, is a point against the actual danger of intrusion of extra-sensory perception as an uncontrolled factor.

7

Dr. J. G. Pratt was one of our most valuable ESP investigators at Duke, and when Dr. Gardner Murphy, of Columbia, generously volunteered his co-operation in extending the scope of the Duke experiments, Pratt was invited to work with him at Columbia in the attempt to discover good ESP subjects there and continue the research. For a long time Pratt's search seemed destined to be unsuccessful. Now and then a promising subject would appear, but would either quickly lose the ability first demonstrated or would not be available for further tests. Pratt is an indefatigable worker and before the year was over he had tested about a hundred and twenty-five people. It was then that he found Mrs. M, who seemed to suit his purpose and would hold up through long series of tests.

The work with Mrs. M was done under a condition that was called STM, which Pratt is the first, I believe, to have used. STM means screened touch matching. The subject touches with a pointer one of the five key cards placed underneath an upright

SCREENED TOUCH MATCHING. J. S. WOODRUFF (LEFT) AND C. E. STUART, MEMBERS OF THE STAFF OF THE DUKE PARAPSYCHOLOGY LABORATORY, DEMONSTRATING THE TEST.

screen which comes down to within three inches
of the table at which he and the investigator are
sitting. On the other side of the screen the experimenter can see the pointer touching the card and
from a pack of cards held in his hand he lays the
top card opposite the key card indicated by the
pointer. Thus the subject can go on pointing as
fast as the experimenter lays down the cards or
as slowly as he desires. In later experiments and in
all present work the table area behind the three-
inch aperture in the screen is completely closed off
from the subject's view by a backboard slightly
higher than the opening and a few inches back from
the screen, on the experimenter's side. One of the
interesting points which Pratt discovered is that this
subject not only could read, but read aloud, while
continuing the touch matching successfully.

Out of a great mass of work which Pratt conducted with Mrs. M he reports at present only
that which he feels confident could not be in any
remote way explainable by anything but the hypothesis of extra-sensory perception. In this experimentation the conditions were very rigid. There
were five shallow pasteboard boxes on the table in
front of the subject, just under the screen arranged
for the key cards. In each of these was one of the
five symbols on a card, face down, covered by a
blank card. These cards had been placed in the
boxes while they were held by Pratt on his knees
below the level of the table. He himself did not

know the arrangement of the symbols in the boxes. Packs of cards were then shuffled by him behind the screen and one by one placed opposite these key-card boxes as the subject indicated with the pointer her choice for each card. The work was done rapidly, at an average rate of about 2.5 cards per second. The subject might or might not be reading a book or she might be carrying on a lively conversation.

Although the results in this technique were by no means among the highest in scoring rate that Pratt obtained from Mrs. M, the experiment was selected merely because of its scientific quality; it still meets the requirements for significant indication of the operation of something beyond chance. The average was only 5.6 hits per 25, but the number of trials in this experiment was 7,800.

Before this manuscript finally left my hands, four other contributions were added to support the case for ESP, a fifth turned out to be a failure, and several other colleges had begun research. I know of several graduate theses on the subject. If my impression is correct, there will be a rapid growth of collegiate interest in the subject, and this if well directed may lead to a hastening of our final understanding of the nature of the process. It is particularly suitable for student research since the techniques are not difficult and the problems are many and interesting.

8

The responsibility, then, for maintaining the case for ESP no longer rests exclusively with Duke. By this time it is a greatly divided one, and I, for one, am immensely relieved. If there is a snag somewhere in the research, at least it has now been overlooked by a good number of qualified observers.

In reviewing only the work done in schools and colleges by academic investigators I have touched on scarcely half of the total amount that has been done. Other teachers besides psychologists have been interested in this work and have busied themselves to see what they could find by the use of the same methods. Some of their work has, indeed, been among the best in every respect. If it has not been pushed forward in publication, it is only because on an already debatable subject hostile criticism will naturally seize on whatever weakness it may find; and such work, though it may not possess weakness, may appear to have it. The fact that a Mr. Smith carried out a series of investigations in a private home does not sound so impressive, unfortunately, as to say that Professor Jones did the same thing in a college laboratory. As a matter of fact, Mr. Smith may be just as good an investigator, or even a better one. He may be more careful, on the whole. Such a comparison is hard to weigh and hard to state. But after all, academic assurances, degrees, and positions do carry weight; and in breaking news of this kind to a doubting world such weight has to be regarded, at least in the initial stages of the research.

Some good work has been done by nonpsychological teachers in colleges, even though it cannot be described by the magic words "carried out in the Psychology Laboratory at ———— College." Much more has been done in private homes with a set of conditions arranged through our instructions, but again lacking the imprimatur of the laboratory. When the smoke of the first scrimmage with the critics dies down sufficiently to permit its proper consideration, much of this work will be highly regarded. Indeed, a lot of it has been done by professional men: physicians, engineers, teachers, or first-rate businessmen. This research by laymen has been done in especially close co-operation with our laboratory, and in most instances a validation procedure has been carried out. For instance, we have had investigators from this laboratory go out to witness experiments, or better, to make actual investigations with the same subjects. In some cases subjects have been brought to the laboratory for the validation. And other methods have been used.

Some of the best scouts for good subjects have been among these unacademic investigators. A highly sociable, enthusiastic young businessman or salesman or a physician practiced in the art of getting co-operation from people is, on the whole, more likely to succeed in finding subjects than is a more formal, and perhaps a little too intellectual, academic person. Certainly the unacademic group has had proportionately greater success than the academic in terms of percentage of good subjects discovered and validated by later investigation.

The future of ESP research in America, then, seems assured. At least forty independent investigators are at work in some way or another and with some degree of contact with our own laboratory. As the center of such a network it is highly important, I believe, that the Duke Parapsychology Laboratory not only continue its own research program, but help to keep a certain amount of standardization of procedure within this large group of outside workers. At the same time we ourselves need to advance further into the several divergent lines already opened up by this research. Along with the increasing opportunity of our work there is, therefore, a feeling among us of greatly increased responsibility.

CHAPTER X

The Investigation of Pure Telepathy

SO FAR IN THIS BOOK THERE HAS BEEN LITTLE mention of telepathy, and though in the popular mind and in the newspaper stories our experiments in extra-sensory perception are usually referred to as experiments in telepathy, this is not strictly true. A large majority of our tests have had nothing to do with telepathy as such. Telepathy is the apprehension by one mind of what is going on in another, or the extra-sensory perception of mental states, thoughts, or whatever you wish to call them. What we have been considering in this book has been principally the extra-sensory perception of objects, mainly cards. This we have been calling "clairvoyance" and would prefer to call "telesthesia."

Most people seem to find it much easier to accept the idea of telepathy than that of clairvoyance. This may be because of the analogy often drawn between radio transmission and the brain-wave theory; that is, the idea that the brain of one person broadcasts and that of another receives, in telepathy. While this is a good analogy upon which to make easy an acceptance of telepathy, it is probably a false one, as will appear later on. Many people have told me that, if necessary, they could accept telepathy as plausible enough, but clairvoyance seemed to them impossible. Telepathy and clairvoyance are two experimentally separate forms of extra-sensory perception, and before the end of this chapter is reached it ought to be clear that one is just as easy to believe (or disbelieve) as the other.

2

Most of the earlier experiments in extra-sensory perception were called experiments in telepathy, but as a matter of fact we do not know whether they were actually that or not. This, because in all those experiments the agent, or sender, had before him an object, a drawing, a number, or a playing card. While he concentrated his attention on this object, the percipient tried to guess or to "see" what he was concentrating on, and it is a question whether success was due to perception of the object or of the thought process of the sender. On the assumption that it was the thought process of the sender, such results in the past were called evidence for telepathy, and the chance that it could equally well have been the object itself was disregarded. The early experimenters did not realize how much of an assumption they were making, for they were not alive to the possibility of clairvoyance in such cases.

As we understand the matter now, such undifferentiated tests as these—which we now call general ESP tests—are useful mainly for exploratory purposes. Perhaps a subject may be able to score better if he is exposed to both the clairvoyant and the telepathic influence at the same time. But so far we have not been able to demonstrate clearly whether or not it makes any fundamental difference when only one process is used, or both. In our work we had used this general ESP condition in the initial tests made by Dr. Lundholm and myself. But in a short time I realized the necessity for a clear separation of the two supposed capacities—telepathy and clairvoyance.

Before I had experimented long with Linzmayer I found that he did not rely on the thought processes of the sender, and when he was asked whether he desired the co-operation of an agent he said that he did not. Similarly, in the early experiments with Pearce, if he knew that the experimenter was looking at the cards the results actually fell almost to chance. This must have been merely because the idea was a distraction at first or because he imagined it would be a hindrance. We find in many cases that a subject's preformed beliefs offer real barriers to his success.

In Pearce's case when we returned later to a renewed trial of general ESP—after he had heard some discussion as to the possible advantage of a combination of telepathy and clairvoyance—he succeeded in scoring higher than he ever had with clairvoyance alone. In two instances he scored 17 out of 25 and once made 15 hits almost in succession. At the same time on alternating runs in which I did not look at the cards he scored only about 7. I thought that this might possibly be due to his having in the meantime come to think there might be some help in the telepathic factor.

The proper step to take next seemed to be to work with the cards behind a screen and in some instances for the experimenter to look at the card and in others not to do so, without letting the subject know the reason. He would merely be told that in some runs the experimenter would look at the cards and in some he would not. But even under these circumstances the results were better under general ESP. Without the possibility of telepathy the average was 8.3; with telepathy the average was 9.7. Later work with another subject, however, has led to the speculation that perhaps even behind the screen the subject may have been aware by extra-sensory perception of which cards were being looked at and may have been stimulated a little more during the periods in which the cards were being seen. Other experimenters have not found the general ESP condition better than the BT (before touching) technique in which the card is called before the investigator removes it from the top of the pack. This technique is a test for clairvoyance

only; therefore, in spite of the results with Pearce,
the value of a telepathic factor added to clairvoyance is still undetermined.

3

By the time our experiments had reached this
point it was clearly essential to test for pure telepathy, and Pearce was the logical man on whom to
try it. The technique itself was difficult to develop.
It seemed advisable to continue using the same symbols so that comparison could be made between
telepathy and clairvoyance. But it was not possible
to choose the symbols from anything objective or
else we might have a basis for an alternate interpretation—possible clairvoyance. Even a coding system
could be open to question on this point. It was decided to begin with the following scheme: The
sender, or agent, selected in his mind a given order
for the symbols in his first five trials—let us say
rectangle, star, rectangle, waves, waves. Keeping
this symbol order dimly in mind, he would concentrate his attention on the first one and signal for
the receiver, or percipient, to make a call. After
the receiver had made his call and it had been
recorded, then and only then would the sender make
the record of his first symbol. In this way there
would be no objective record until after the receiver's call was recorded. Clairvoyance from the
record would not be possible unless we suppose it

ST FOR PURE TELEPATHY. MR. ZIRKLE WAS SEATED TWO ROOMS AWAY
M THE SENDER, MISS OWNBEY, WITH HIS BACK TOWARD HER. THE
GRAPH KEY UNDER MISS OWNBEY'S RIGHT HAND WAS USED TO GIVE
READY SIGNAL. UNDER THESE CONDITIONS MR. ZIRKLE GOT 23 HITS
OF 25, 85 OUT OF 100, AND AN AVERAGE FOR THE SERIES OF 16
OUT OF 25.

capable of going ahead into the future. Therefore, after the first five symbols were called, the next five would be chosen with some systematic variation, which system in itself would be varied so as to offset completely any guessing of the order.

At first Pearce did poorly. His scores averaged little above 6. But as he went on he improved until his average rose almost to 8 per 25. As a matter of fact his perceptivity varied with different senders. With two young ladies his average rose to 8.7, which was almost equal to his general average for the clairvoyant card work.

Most of our early telepathy tests were made with sender and receiver seated at the same table. The receiver would not look at the sender, but there was a continual possibility of auditory cues such as clearing the throat, scraping chairs, or fidgeting about in general. After a time, however, a noisy electric fan was used as a block to possible auditory cues, although it is extremely doubtful if any such cues were operative or whether a scraping chair could indicate a star rather than a circle, and so on. It is practically certain that no such cues were being utilized, since most of the subjects did equally well, if not better, later when they were separated from the sender by walls and distance.

Miss Bailey in particular did better when she was at a distance from the sender. She showed ability in telepathy from the start, but increased her scoring average when she was separated from the sender in an adjoining room and did still better when located two rooms away. In most cases when our subjects were in separate rooms the connecting doors were left at least partly open. Distance and separation certainly had a favorable rather than an unfavorable effect on most of the scores. Whatever the means of communication between the two minds engaged in the tests, nothing in the way of unconscious sensory cues could explain that increasing success which attended separation.

In the majority of trials under these conditions the electric fan was going and in some an experimenter was in the middle room between sender and receiver where he could to best advantage catch any sounds or signals.

The greatest amount of really amazing work in telepathy was performed by Zirkle, and it was done during the period when Miss Ownbey was both sender and experimenter. At first the work was done with both subject and experimenter in the same room, but later with the receiver one and then two rooms away from the sender, with open doors between. Throughout the duration of the test the electric fan was going and Zirkle sat with his back to the experimenter. His eyes were closed and his mind was adjusted to the greatest degree of abstraction of which he was capable in the normal waking state. The ready signal, or notice that the sender was concentrating on a new card, was given by means of a telegraphic sounder. The receiver

called his choice aloud; the experimenter recorded
it, and if correct, checked it. We recognized that
this procedure placed a great deal of responsibility
on the observer, and if this work of the Zirkles' stood
alone, unsupported by any from other subjects and
other experimenters, it might make the precautions
appear inadequate. There was, however, a great deal
of independent support. These experiments were
devoted primarily to the understanding of relations
and conditions of extra-sensory perception in subjects who had already demonstrated its possession.
To have supplied another observer was beyond our
means at the time.

4

During the course of his work on pure telepathy
Zirkle gave us our finest demonstration of the effect
of sodium amytal on ESP. At the same time we
were able to study the effect of caffeine, which is
the active stimulant principle in coffee and tea. The
two drugs were given to Zirkle without his knowing which one he was taking; he knew, of course,
that the amytal was expected to depress his scoring, because he knew about its effect on previous
subjects, and he knew, too, that caffeine might raise
the scoring capacity of a subject depressed by fatigue. As a psychology student he understood that
in their effect on mental processes these two drugs
work against each other to a great extent: if amytal
makes a person sleepy, caffeine makes him wide

awake. Amytal tends to dissociate a subject; caffeine helps to reintegrate him or pull him together mentally.

Because Zirkle knew all these facts we had to adopt the precaution of not letting him know which drug he was taking, and the capsules in which they were put up looked alike. However, the general effects of each drug were so pronounced that he had small trouble in recognizing which he had taken by the way he began to feel shortly after the dose. Nor would any observer have been uncertain as to when Zirkle had had the sleep-producing drug and when the stimulant.

We had worked with caffeine before in the case of Pearce. Its use had considerably raised his averages at times when he was scoring unusually low, but it never raised his scoring above his usual or normal level. This suggested that its principal effect was to offset the results of fatigue. Ordinarily Pearce's below-normal runs had come on days when he had been up late the night before. From our observations on Pearce we thought it probable that if amytal brought down the level of Zirkle's scores on this occasion, caffeine might bring him back to his normal level.

Miss Ownbey was the sender and experimenter in this particular series, and it was the first time that amytal and caffeine had been used in work on pure telepathy. Zirkle was stationed in one room and Miss Ownbey in another. As was customary, she used a telegraph key to signal when she was ready. Zirkle had been averaging 13.6 hits in each run of 25 trials before he took the first amytal dosage. After waiting an hour for it to take effect, the tests were resumed. Zirkle's average had fallen to 7.8, the first series being composed of 300 trials. Two hours after taking the first capsule he would drop asleep between tests if he was not interfered with. He was seeing double and felt dizzy. After the third hour, when he took a third test of 300 runs, he felt worse than ever and his average was down to only 6.2 hits in each 25 calls.

We felt that this was the time to try the effect of caffeine. Everyone who has used a cup of strong coffee to wake himself up (or sober himself) knows about what the second capsule did to Zirkle. An hour after he had taken it his scores were up to an average of 9.5 in 25 calls. Unfortunately he could not stay for a second series of 300 an hour after the first postcaffeine runs, but he reported later that he went on being more and more wide awake.

Some time after Miss Ownbey and Zirkle were married we conducted another group of telepathy tests with them. This time a third person acted as recorder, taking down Zirkle's calls in a separate room and keeping an independent record. Although the results were not equal to the high level of 14 hits or thereabouts which Zirkle had been able to score before his marriage, he did average 9 hits in each 25 calls—far above the chance figure.

5

In describing these tests for telepathy and clairvoyance it is easy to overlook their implications and
the excitement that was an inevitable part of them.
This narrative will carry more conviction if it is
factual and restrained, and yet there were moments
in our researches when it was impossible not to be
deeply stirred by the almost incredible nature of
what was happening. One such moment occurred
during a special test for telepathy, with Miss Ownbey as the sender and Miss Turner as the receiver.

What made this test remarkable was the distance
between the two subjects. Miss Turner was two
hundred and fifty miles away from Miss Ownbey
and the Duke laboratory. The experiment was
arranged for a daily run of 25 calls, with an inter-
val of five minutes after each call, so that each
daily test occupied two hours. The two subjects
used synchronized watches based on Western Union
time. Miss Ownbey turned in to me the records of
the order in which she had sent out the symbols,
mentally, and these I retained to check against Miss
Turner's calls, which were to be mailed to me.

Apparently the instructions to Miss Turner went
astray, for the records of her first three days' calls
were mailed to Miss Ownbey, who brought them
straight from the post office to me. The letter containing them was entirely in Miss Turner's hand-
writing, and subsequent investigation convinced

me that it had not been tampered with. Placing Miss Ownbey's records of the symbols she had attempted to send out to Miss Turner against the calls which Miss Turner had listed in her letter, scores of 19 hits for the first day and 16 each for the next two days were revealed. A three-day average of above 17 correct impressions of the images in Miss Ownbey's mind out of a possible 25.

To many people there must appear something fantastic in such results. They will think of the hills, woods, towns, fields, roads, rivers, even of the very curve of the earth itself separating the two women who conducted this experiment. And yet two times out of three one of them knew what was the shape of an image held in the thought of the other. Whatever power it was that they possessed, it plainly was totally unaffected by distance, for these three scores were among the highest ever attained in our work on telepathy. Space as ordinarily conceived in our everyday thinking presented no obstacle, then, to telepathic communication of symbols.

It is possible that we made a mistake after receiving those first three phenomenal scores from Miss Turner. Because the trials at five-minute intervals took so long, we shortened the time between calls. Also, possibly unwisely, we let Miss Turner know how high her scores had run. For succeeding days she was able to make hits of only 7, 7, 8, 6, and 2 successively. Still, for the entire series her average was 10.1 for each 25 calls, or more than twice as much as chance would ordinarily produce.

Against the evidence of this particular series of successful runs must be set the fact that when we tried a further number of runs nothing encouraging happened. And Zirkle—whose scores, as stated above, actually improved with increases in distance up to 30 feet—when attempting a series of telepathic tests with Miss Ownbey at a distance of 165 miles was able to score no better than a chance average. Certainly a great deal of work remains to be done in this field.

6

In our experiments as a whole, however, we have generally neglected telepathy. This has been largely for the reason that it is difficult to control so as to leave no possible alternative explanation. In the first place, one has two subjects to keep track of, the sender and the receiver. Second, there is a possibility that two people may have or may acquire similar order habits: may tend to start off a run with the same symbol and to follow in some particular routine order. But we think we have a way of avoiding that, and actual checkup shows that we do. Miss Ownbey's records prove that she does avoid routine patterns. Also, a cross-check between her records and those of Miss Turner, checking together records that were not intended to go together, gives a close approximation to 5, as expected by chance. This shows that the two were not following simply in the same habitual order. Our present instructions in using this technique depend upon employing a pack of cards with a memorized and unrecorded code. The pack of cards will have on it only a set of numbers from 1 to 5 to represent symbols, with only the sender knowing which symbols they stand for in his mind.

Therefore, while I consider our results in telepathy perfectly good, standing as they do against the background of the more firmly founded card work, yet I am sure that we have been wise in concentrating major attention on the case for ESP of the clairvoyant, or objective, type. If the work is correct, we have for the first time in the history of the subject experimentally separated telepathy and clairvoyance. Further, we have shown that there is a process of telepathy and that it works under conditions in which there is no objective record (unless thought process is itself objective) and that clairvoyance is possible without the interoperation of telepathy.

After all the labor of experimental separation, it would appear now that these two phenomena, telepathy and clairvoyance, which we have shown to be different in their experimental demonstration, are basically probably closely related, if not really expressions of the same fundamental process. All the major subjects whom we have tried in the one set of tests have been able also to succeed in the other. Those who are telepathic are also clairvoyant, and vice versa.

' This is more than coincidence. Suppose our estimate of only one person in five having ESP ability should be a fair one; to find eight good clairvoyant subjects thus selected and eight good telepathic subjects to be the same individuals would be most improbable by chance alone. But when we add to this the fact that these subjects are tested for the two capacities during the same general period—when we get closely comparable scores on both telepathy and clairvoyance—we find that the subject does nearly as well in the one as in the other. Five out of our eight major subjects scored within one point of the same average in both telepathy and clairvoyance. In some instances, where fluctuations from day to day were on record, the fluctuations would take in general the same trend in both telepathy and clairvoyance. Conditions which affected the one affected the other in every instance in which we have such records. Sodium amytal lowered clairvoyance and lowered telepathy. The effect of caffeine was the same on both. Mild respiratory illnesses such as colds and influenza operated similarly. Distance tests had the same effect on both. Not a single differentiating fact is available. The only subject tested thoroughly in whom we found any marked difference between the two capacities was Mrs. Garrett, and since her case is a very special one it deserves separate treatment in a later chapter.

There seems to be, then, reason to believe that extra-sensory perception is a general process of which telepathy and clairvoyance are special forms, that the differentiating characteristic is simply that different orders of things are perceived: in the case of telepathy, a thought; in the case of clairvoyance, a symbol on a card. This may be regarded as at least a good working hypothesis.

The history of physics now reveals to us the importance which lay in the first linkages of what were earlier regarded as independent phenomena: the linkage of sound with motion, of heat with work, of electricity with light, and so forth. Has parapsychology made its first experimentally demonstrated linkage? Perhaps it is too soon to be sure; the phenomena of this field are far more complex, and certainly far more difficult to relate to each other, than are those of the physical realm.

CHAPTER XI

The General Mental Setting

THE PRECEDING CHAPTER SUGGESTED THAT SOME-
how or other clairvoyance and telepathy fit together. The next step is to find where they belong in
the psychological scheme of things. What is the
relation of extra-sensory perception to the rest of
the mind?

Most of the work in ESP investigation has been
of a fact-finding nature. Many more years of factual research will be needed before we have enough
data to form complete hypotheses. The powers or
energies of the mind are enormously complex, and
even its most "normal" manifestations are incom-
pletely understood by modern psychologists. Yet
with all these reservations it is possible to say that
a beginning has been made in bringing order and
relationship into the study of ESP. The discovery
of a close connection between telepathy and clairvoyance represents one step in that direction.

In addition to forming an outline for further
study in a new field and attempting to find relationships between its facts, it is a most important
advance to be able to relate the new subject to the
existing body of knowledge. In the case of ESP

an important connection between it and established scientific knowledge is at once apparent. For the extra-sensory modes of perception are not completely isolated, discordant mental activities. They appear to be part of the normal make-up of the human mind, even though they are sharply differentiated from the type of perception which we call sensory. In other words, they are in many respects related to better known and more fully studied aspects of psychology.

2

In trying to fit the discoveries that have been made about the process of extra-sensory perception into the general scientific picture of the mind, one disclaimer should, in fairness, be entered at this point. Our task in doing so would be much less difficult if academic psychology, on its part, were a further developed science than it is. If more were known about the common processes of the mind, such as thinking, willing, feeling, remembering, and the like, we might be able more successfully to relate the ESP process to them. Having entered the field of psychology with a training and background in the older branches of study, including chemistry, physiology, and botany, I cannot fail to be appalled at the predominance of insecure method and of unverified speculation and assumption in psychology today. For many besides myself the tendency of the work in modern psychology to coagulate into a multitude of small schools, each created and stimulated by strong leadership, must be a depressing matter.

In justice to my fellow psychologists (whom I have perhaps adopted with greater equanimity than they can muster in adopting me) it needs to be said that they have problems to solve and conditions to contend with which are incomparably more complicated and perplexing than those of the biological and physical sciences. I maintain emphatically that the men and women who are working in psychology today are as brilliant and competent a corps as any of the other sciences can boast. But the science of psychology (if it may be so described) suffers from the peculiar difficulties of its problems and the reluctance of those who are exploring them to abandon either the old guardrails of philosophy or the alluring analogies of other and more advanced sciences.

Whatever may be the reason, our psychology, our knowledge of the human mind, has not yet reached the point where we can make precise statements of general principles in the field. How, then, can we determine where and how the findings of the research in ESP are to be placed in the general system of the mind? I believe we can take only tentative steps in this direction, and if the relations are somewhat loosely connected and unspecific, psychology as a whole must share the blame.

3

To begin with, there are certain positive relations and certain negative ones that may be pointed out between extra-sensory perception and other processes of the mind. Turning first to some of the positive ones, I would point to the fact that ESP is clearly a part of the general activity of the mental system. That is, there is every evidence that ESP functions jointly with the other processes of the mind and is not separate and independent.

If a subject calls a pack of cards, for example, a great many mental processes besides ESP help him to identify the pack, to understand what the general purpose of the experiment is, and so on. Then, memory retains the five symbols and judgment distinguishes them; imagination, too, may be involved in keeping the five symbols clearly "before the mind" when the subject calls one of the symbols, or there may be a motor response when the subject places a card opposite one of the key cards, as in the technique of matching described in a previous chapter. And so ESP, whatever it may be, is at any rate a part of the general complex process-system that we call the mind or, to be still more inclusive, of the personality as a whole.

It might be added further that this process or phenomenon of ESP is clearly voluntary, or capable of being directed; like other mental processes, even though we have difficulty in bringing it completely under control. One illustration of this power of direction is that a subject calls the order of the cards in the particular pack with which he happens to be working, and not the order of some other pack in the laboratory or elsewhere. He calls it, too, at a certain time, at a certain rate, and in a certain way. He may begin at the bottom or the top, or stop halfway through if he wishes. Hardly anything could more plainly identify the extra-sensory perceptive capacity with the total organization of the mind, as an integral part of its natural order, than this relatively complete control exercised by the subject himself. He can even call so as to miss the symbol on a particular card, or he may make two calls, one aiming to hit and the other aiming to miss. If he has the ability to call a high score he can reverse the direction on the next run and obtain a correspondingly low score.

ESP requires the attention of the subject. It is necessary for him to concentrate on the task. Along with this concentration of attention must go also freedom from distraction. Both are aspects of the same process and, although psychologists disagree greatly as to what attention is or whether there is any specific mental process under that heading, everyone knows pretty well what it means.

We have noted the effect of lack of concentration when we described the work of various subjects. Strange observers brought in to scrutinize the subject proved to be distracting. With Pearce this invariably brought his scores down to an average of chance until he became accustomed to their presence and was able again to concentrate on the tests. It may also be remembered that new techniques distracted him, disturbing the state of deep absorption into which he naturally lapsed when engaged in calling the cards. Another subject once warned me that he was afraid he could not do very well so long as a certain young lady was in town. She attracted him greatly and distracted him from anything else. And as a matter of fact his scoring did fall considerably lower during the period of her stay. Once when Cooper received a disturbing telephone call in the midst of a series his score on returning from the telephone was a 3. That was unusually low for him.

Some subjects, like Mrs. M in the Columbia experiments, can divide their attention much as a person does in playing the piano and singing at the same time or in doing needlework while listening to a lecture or to music. In such cases there is no real interference with attention, but rather distribution or division of it. It therefore appears that some subjects can do ESP best under conditions of divided attention. Also, as we have already mentioned, attention is easier at the beginning and end of a run, just as it is in the memorizing of a column of figures.

One of the most striking similarities between extra-sensory perception and other difficult mental processes is the need in the case of both for confidence. Few people can perform a difficult feat of physical skill without confidence. The least doubt crossing the mind of a high jumper or of a trapeze performer may be fatal to his success. This is equally if not more markedly true with delicate mental skills and creative work. Performance, especially in the arts, is dependent upon confidence. Fine discriminative judgment, in the laboratory and out of it, is largely dependent upon confidence. In ESP work judgment, of course, functions on an extrasensory instead of a sensory basis.

That confidence is essential to ESP is very apparent in the failures that come when a new and apparently difficult condition is imposed upon a subject, as when Pearce was first tested for telepathy. At first the subject fails, but later, with encouragement and growing confidence, he succeeds. Zirkle began by failing flatly in clairvoyance, although he had been getting high results in telepathy. He had no confidence in his ability to score clairvoyantly. Cooper failed just as completely on distance work at first, though much later, with a sender in whom he had the greatest confidence, he did very well. It is not possible to say, of course, that lack of confidence was the only factor in all these cases. A conclusion here should be quite tentative, but the effect of encouragement from a little success is to bring greater success; on the other hand, the depressing effect of failure is one of the most marked general impressions which one gets from watching subjects work from day to day.

Sometimes a subject will score well even though beginning with strong doubt of the whole research. Miss Ownbey was such a subject. But presumably a person who can "play the game," or enter into the test wholeheartedly, may for the moment lay aside her doubts and escape her limitations. Few people, however, can do this freely, and I feel that confidence is important. My own view is that Miss Ownbey was nearer to believing in ESP than she realized. This opinion is based partly on her account of family experiences of an extra-sensory nature, which doubtless left some impression on her.

There is apparently no surer way of bringing down ESP scores than by causing nervous dissociation. Whether this dissociation is the result of narcotic drugs, extreme fatigue, or sleepiness probably does not matter. There are other ways of producing it that probably would have the same result. In this respect ESP is closely parallel to reasoning, creative thinking, and judgment in general. It is well known that nervous dissociation, most often observed through the influence of narcotic drugs, impairs the judgment. Alcohol is the commonest drug producing such impairment of judgment. We have noted that in the use of sodium amytal extra-sensory perception is interfered with before sensory perception, just as judgment is impaired before the senses are. In its general reactions, then, ESP belongs more distinctly with the higher mental processes than it does with the lower. But again this may be due to the fact that specific judgment is involved in each call. That is, we may still not have touched the peculiar character of a more elemental and basic process. It is best not to be too satisfied with what may be only a superficial relationship.

4

Capacity for ESP declines when interest declines. This has been indicated in the decline curves of Stuart, and also in the longer drawn-out decline of Linzmayer. But it may also be observed within the period of a single sitting when children are being tested. The outward signs of interest in a child are easily recognized. As these overt symptoms indicate a decline of interest, the falling off in scoring may be depended upon to follow almost surely.

Interest, however, is a very general term. The interest of the subject may be of a number of different kinds: At first it may be an interest in the tests, in seeing how well he can do. Such interest is a more personal and vital one. Later this may give way to an intellectual interest in how the work is going in general and what it may mean scientifically or philosophically. Such interest is of little use in promoting actual high scoring. It is the fresh, original, personal interest that is important for success, much like the interest one shows in a game.

5

Those of us who have been working for several years with ESP subjects have been coming gradually to feel that our chief problem is to get the subject to let go of his natural inhibitions, his mental habits that are so bound up with rational and sensory processes. In this respect, again, good conditions for the ESP subject are quite similar to good conditions for the learning of an act of skill or an art or for entering into a group activity. The person who is inhibited, who cannot let himself go and play the game, is likely to be unsuccessful in both types of activity. Inhibitions, too, are internal interferences with concentration of attention, and the effective work that normally follows it.

Summing up this brief survey, the reader will see that extra-sensory perception is most like the higher, more complex mental processes in the conditions it requires and the relationships it shows. It has also, of course, many differences from these so-called higher mental activities, but in common it has the elements of judgment, of concentration of attention with freedom from distraction, need for an active and sustained interest and confidence and for a good state of nervous integration. It is a voluntary activity directed and controlled, in-hibited or released in general much as are those processes of mind which are already somewhat familiar.

6

So much for what extra-sensory perception is like and what it is related to. But it does not fit in as harmoniously with all the other properties of mind as it does with the higher mental processes. There are some things that it is emphatically unlike. The chief of these is *sensory* perception. At the beginning of our research we used the expression "extra-sensory perception," meaning perception beyond the *recognized senses*. But every year since the work began I have become more convinced that ESP is fundamentally different from sense perception, and extra-sensory has come to mean *outside* the senses in every respect.

I feel that on this point there is much stronger evidence than on the positive relations just described. In ESP there seems to be no discoverable localization. No subject knows where an ESP impression hits him. Nor does he know when it hits him. There is no local area that is recognizable as better than another to turn toward the card or the sender. Backs are as good as fronts, feet as good as heads, so far as anyone through all the experimental history of the subject has reliably discovered.

Of course, there have been people who talked about the solar plexus and others who want to hold the card to their foreheads, and there are various

kinds of claims for nonocular vision which emphasize some special part of the skin or body as serving
best for this purpose. But from such acquaintance
as I have had with these theories there is no reliable
experimental basis for any of their claims. When
someone specifies that he has to see through his nos-
trils or from his temple or cheekbone, I think that
is the most likely place to look for inadequate ex-
clusion of sensory cues. No such claims have been
made by any of our subjects, and almost every conceivable angle of the body has been turned toward
the card or the sender without interfering with success. And no amount of introspection can localize
any part of the periphery or interior of the body at
which there is a reliable feeling of reception such as
one has when pain, temperature, and other sensory
stimuli are given to the nerves of a particular area.

7

ESP stands by itself on another score. It does not
matter how the object to be perceived is held, at
what angle or in what position. It seems highly
probable, too, that the range of objects perceptible
in ESP is relatively unlimited. Indeed, there is hardly
a wider range conceivable than that which lies between the order of a pack of cards, on the one
hand, and the mental states of a distant person, on
the other. All the senses taken together do not range
so widely.

To emphasize a difference between ESP and the recognized senses which has already been pointed out, sensory perception resists the effect of narcotic drugs long after extra-sensory perception is blotted out. The same thing is true of the effect of excitement, distraction, and perhaps many other things. While under the influence of a drug Zirkle's ESP capacity was reduced almost to chance level from his previous extremely high scoring but he could still read and hear and feel pain. Even Linzmayer with his higher drug dosage could still hear me quite plainly, could see what the cards were in the checkup, and although he could not walk straight, he was clearly aware of his disequilibrium. Therefore, there seems a clear margin between sensory and extra-sensory perception.

There lies in the very nature of the test itself an obvious but most important distinction. For perception by the senses the symbol is printed on the "wrong side of the card." That is, in a test such as the down-through technique, the subject has to perceive the symbol on the bottom cards through the other cards or else through the table, whichever is easier. Still further, when stone walls and other obstacles are put in the way, on the sensory analogy, perception has to go through them or else around the corner. An apparent independence of barriers, therefore, marks a difference that is easily overlooked, because from the beginning the tests have to exclude the senses.

8

The sharpest distinction of all between sensory and extra-sensory perception tests is that none of the senses show any such relative independence of distance or space relations as seems to hold with ESP. As a matter of fact, only a part of our senses surmounts distance at all, and those do so at a sacrifice of clarity with distance. The farther away the object seen or source of the sound heard, the poorer the sensation will be. Not so ESP, as we shall see in considerable detail in the chapter that follows.

The effect of distance binds up with it a number of other points which a complete description would have to include. For instance, distance and size are related. If by extra-sensory perception a distant object can be perceived just as well as a close one, ought not a small one be perceived as well as a large one? Work which Mrs. Rhine has conducted with a group of neighborhood children, and a report of which she has recently published, bears out the logical prediction on this point. Her work also shows some other contrasts between ESP and normal sensory perception.

Finally, in all the sensory relations which the personality has with the world we have found through the advance of physical science that there is an intermediate process relation, some sort of causal energy. In all cases of sensory perception, forms of energy have been found appropriate to the particular sense organ concerned: light energy for the eye, sound energy for the ear, chemical energy transformations for the senses of taste and smell. The next chapter will make clear that there is no known form of energy to convey ESP impressions to wherever in the body they are perceived.

A backward glance shows that at many points ESP fits into certain common relationships with higher processes of mind, and that it seems to be a normal part of the integral system of mind. It does not belong under the heading of sensory perception, however, nor is it a sixth or a seventh or an nth sense. This may possibly be hard to accept for many readers who feel that they must have some kind of hypothesis as a handrail. All I can say is that there will probably soon be plenty of hypotheses, but they must be framed out of the facts obtained from experimentation rather than from old and untested assumptions based on the inadequate facts of the past. Better, I think (following Newton), not to try too hastily to explain untested theoretical commitments and, keeping one's objectives and safeguards clearly in mind, to search for the answers, in further experiments, from the facts themselves.

CHAPTER XII

Physical Relationships

PERHAPS THE OLDEST OF ALL OUR SCIENCES IS physics, which is concerned with matter and energy. Investigation into its problems has been carried on for many centuries. But although hundreds of years before Christ men were already making simple discoveries about matter and motion and principles of practical importance, the really scientific era of physics begins with Galileo's famous experiment in which he dropped weights from the leaning tower of Pisa.

Whether, as so many people believe, physics is the most basic of all our natural sciences will depend, I should judge, on whether the universe is basically physical. We may find that out in time, but we do not know it now. Nevertheless, this branch of science appears to have penetrated so far into its former mysteries that it is now something of a standard, a natural frame of reference for the other sciences. About any new phenomenon one wants to know what are its relations to physics and where, if at all, it belongs in the complex system of mechanical law that this elaborate science has constructed. What place, then, if any, can be found for extra-sensory perception in the field of physics?

It is illuminating to notice that in the history of extra-sensory investigation the most interested of the scientists have been the physicists. We think at once of Sir Oliver Lodge, Sir William Barrett, and Sir William Crookes. There are other great Englishmen too—Lord Rayleigh, Sir William Ramsay, and Sir J. J. Thomson. Among the Germans we can add the names of Einstein, Ostwald, and the Austrian, Mach. All these men have proposed a theory or in some other way turned their attention to the infant science of parapsychology, and in the response elicited by the Duke experiments from the scientific world the physicists have taken a prominent place.

2

Hospitable as the physicists themselves have been to the investigation of extra-sensory perception, the science of physics itself has been quite the contrary. In spite of all efforts to link ESP with the world of physical processes, which science understands so relatively thoroughly, there appears to be no known physical condition or process to which it can be related. Naturally, whatever we mean by the term "extra-sensory perception," it is a part of our physical world in certain respects. There has to be an object to perceive and a person to perceive it, and both the object and the person perceiving it are in the physical realm.

But whatever goes on between the object and the person perceiving it—the perception of the object by the human consciousness—seems to be a process which does not have any characteristic that would identify it with the science of physics, at least so far as we have been able to discover. Physicists who have examined our work, however, rightly insist that the object, the symbol on the card, must mean *something,* and that, since it is a physical entity, physics must play some part in the field we are investigating.

"Right," we must so far reply. "The card symbol is the thing perceived, but is the process by which it enters the conscious knowledge of the percipient, the person who perceives it, in any way a detectably physical process?"

The answer, up to the present, is "no."

"But," say the physicists, "why, then, does it matter whether or not there are symbols on your cards? Why don't you have somebody just think there is a symbol on the card? According to you, it ought to work just as well."

"It does work just as well," we reply, citing the evidence for pure telepathy. "Perhaps that is all that is happening when we have somebody think of a symbol without the card. There is no important difference in the two kinds of result."

"Well," the argument continues, "doesn't thinking itself involve brain action? Then you're still in the realm of physics, dealing with the physical activity of the nerve cells of the brain."

To that our answer must be: "We don't know yet, and will not know until physics advances farther into the study of brain action and finds out what happens when a human mind thinks. Then we shall know whether thought is a wholly physical process or is partially nonphysical, whatever 'nonphysical' may be. Only at that point shall we be able to say whether or not a physical stimulus is necessary for ESP. Then pure telepathy, of course, may prove not to be so 'pure' if there is a physical basis in the brain for all thought patterns."

3

It is important to understand clearly why the processes of extra-sensory perception bear no discoverable relationship to physics. Much of the evidence on this point has been given in previous chapters when we were demonstrating that extra-sensory perception is not like sense perception. The physical world is the world of the senses. Sense data are the foundations of physics; and so the physical world is the world reported to the human mind by the senses and inferred from the data collected by the senses.

The only known physical principle that might conceivably apply to extra-sensory perception is that of radiant energy. If the explanation of ESP is a part of the science of physics as we now understand it, and if the symbol perceived is not communicated directly by any or all of the five recognized senses, then it must be conveyed by some sort of wave or ray.

This radiant energy explanation is a comparatively old hypothesis, almost as old as the scientific study of ESP itself. Back in the last century Sir William Crookes proposed the brain-wave hypothesis of telepathy, which has been mentioned in the third chapter. At the same time German physicists were already speculating on radiant energy theories of telepathy. The great advance of physics into short-wave radiation has, on the one hand, widened the scope of possible relations between ESP and radiant energy, and hence complicated the problem. On the other hand, the analogy of short-wave transmission in radio, which also is able to conquer distance, has overcome for many people the objections that were easily raised in the old days against the brain-wave theory. When it was claimed that telepathy operated at a distance, the assertion ran counter to what was then known of wave energetics.

But a good analogy, although it helps a great deal in popular thought, does not reliably assist the scientist toward his goal of finding out what actually occurs. In this case, if we consider together the results of all the tests that can be brought to bear on the wave theory, the analogy, even with the aid of its modern extensions, and suppositions, seems inadequate.

First, there is the question of the angle at which the card is held. From the physical viewpoint, in order to convey impressions of a figure printed in ink on a white card it would be necessary to fall back on differential radiation or differential absorption. In other words, either the figures on the cards are giving off radiation that is different from that given off by the cards themselves or else radiation coming from a more remote point is absorbed in different degrees by the ink and by the card: theoretically, more would be absorbed by the ink figures than by the card, just as in an X-ray photograph of a ring on one's finger the ring absorbs more of the X rays than the finger does, and therefore registers an impression on the photographic plate upon which the rays impinge. Whether the supposed rays are given off by the ink figures or whether it is merely a case of rays passing through the card and being absorbed more by the ink than by the card, the card would have to be either facing toward or facing away from the subject in order to give him the pattern. If the card were in the same plane ("edgewise" in common terms) as the subject and at a distance, the symbols would be indistinguishable by him, since on either theory of radiation the printed figures would convey only the effect of straight lines.

In the mist of speculation surrounding modern

physics there are certain untested hypotheses that allow for practically anything imaginable. One kind of geometry among the many non-Euclidian systems, for example, is doubtless available in which it would theoretically be better for the card to be turned edgewise to the percipient than broadside on. But there is no rational comfort in using unstable speculations to explain these data. We should consider the facts of radiation mechanics when we compare our results with wave effects, and not rely on sheer imagination. And by all the known wave characteristics applicable to the card phenomena here concerned, the angle of the card to the percipient would be important. When new and different properties of waves are found, then it may be time to reconsider.

When the question of barriers between the object and the percipient is raised, the hypothetical type of very short ray, like the X ray, which is necessary to fill the requirements for an explanation of ESP, will be positively eliminated. If extra-sensory perceptivity were occasioned by something of the character of X or ultraviolet rays, the walls separating the subject from the cards would be effective barriers, especially when there are two or three rooms between, with some little distance thrown in. If one falls back upon an analogy of the cosmic ray, which has much greater penetrating power, he encounters the difficulties of needing to assume sufficient intensity to throw adequate "light." There has to be enough such radiation to throw a shadow by differential absorption. It seems fairly certain that any such radiation coming from ordinary inkwells or card materials would long ago have affected the electric instruments and sensitive plates of the laboratories. Also, even cosmic rays could not penetrate the several hills and mountains lying between Junaluska and Durham, when Miss Turner and Miss Ownbey were carrying on the 250-mile telepathy series. And so the search for a wave type which would fit this theory seems fruitless.

There are certain people who, like a friend of mine, have suggested that since gravitation—whatever it is—penetrates everything known, it might offer a better analogy. Perhaps something like gravitation may be found to fit the facts of ESP, but not the gravitational energy itself. For, though the effect of distance on gravitation is great, it does not affect ESP so far as we can determine. We are not, therefore, encouraged to think that anything like gravitation will explain ESP as the evidence stands at present.

Any radiation theory becomes more difficult still when we raise the question of how one card in a pack of 25, especially at the bottom of the pack, can be distinguished from the others. If there were to be radiation passing through such a pack of cards, the effect would be to produce on the mind of the subject only a summarized blotch or hodge-

podge of twenty-five figures piled on top of each
other, such as a photograph would show if the cards
were stamped with lead and photographed by X
ray. To distinguish one from the other would be
hardly even an imaginable possibility, to say nothing of succeeding best of all with the last five cards
down through, as most subjects have done. Again
one can imagine physical theories that might conceivably allow this, granted more speculations
about the resolving power of the ESP process. But
nothing we *now know* about waves and minds
allows us to apply a wave theory to these results.

4

Besides all these objections, to explain extra-
sensory perception by a wave theory calls for applying the theory not merely to the clairvoyant card
tests, but to telepathy as well. It must apply not
only to the range of *objects* which have been used
successfully in ESP tests (and that range is fairly
wide if the work of others who experimented with
a more diversified range of objects than we did is
included), but it must also be applicable to a *mere
thought* in a human mind. Where are the rays to
come from in this latter case? From the brain, let
us say. But would there be the same kind of transmission or absorption of radiation for the *thought*
of a circle as that which would come from a material object, a card with a circle stamped on it?

It is on the greater difficulty of explaining both clairvoyance and telepathy that theorists have always fallen down in the past.

The next thing to be considered is the distance data—the results obtained from testing subjects at a distance from the cards or from the telepathic sender. Here it must be admitted that the wave theory comes under even more strain. I can think of no greater blow that could be given it than comes from this evidence itself. If it were found that subjects in clairvoyance and telepathy tests did fairly well within a few feet or a few yards of the test material and then fell off as they got farther away, one might suppose that there was some kind of compensating adjustment such as we are accustomed to finding on our modern radios, a sort of volume control. But when a subject does the best work he has done in months when he is separated a hundred yards from the cards, and when another does the best work she has ever done when separated 250 miles from the sender, there is nothing left for a wave theory to work on, and no physicist has ever even argued the point.

The closest analogy so far offered has been that of the skip-distance effect on short-wave radio transmission, in which distance is not so effective in causing a decline of intensity as it is in longer wave lengths. But there are two things wrong even with this analogy: first, the skip-distance phenomenon does show a degree of decline of intensity with

distance; second, and still more important, no analogy with even the shorter radio waves could re-
motely apply to the card situation. These radio
waves are much too long. We would have to have
a really short wave to transmit card symbols, one
measured in very small fractions of millimeters
rather than in meters, and such "really short waves"
would certainly be absorbed in passing 250 miles
along the earth's surface through atmosphere and
houses and mountains. The skip-distance analogy
is apparently of no help in explaining ESP.

Finally—and this is the most important point of
all—these objections to the wave hypothesis have
to be considered together as a cumulative body of
negative testimony. Probably all of them apply in
some measure if not *in toto,* and when they are
taken jointly they appear to leave no ground for
any theory of wave transmission in extra-sensory
perception, so fas as the nature of waves is understood today.

5

The whole body of evidence for ESP at a distance
is not found solely in the Duke experiments. Earlier
instances of distance tests have been reported. By
far the best of these, in my opinion, are the experiments reported by Upton Sinclair in his book *Mental Radio,* experiments which were conducted with
his wife as subject and which won recognition from
such different scientists as Einstein and McDougall.

These experiments by Sinclair are certainly the best that have been conducted outside university laboratories and are written, as might be expected, much more interestingly.

The particular series in question is that carried on with thirty miles intervening between the sender and the receiver, Mrs. Sinclair. Seven drawings were made by Mrs. Sinclair to represent objects on which the sender, who was her brother-in-law, was concentrating his attention thirty miles away, and all were relatively if not completely successful. These results are, of course, not evaluable by statistical method, but the person who examines them can hardly escape the conviction that something besides similar habits of thought and coincidence was responsible. The only point we need to make here is that these seven telepathically stimulated drawings were among the most precise which Mrs. Sinclair was ever able to produce. In other tests she did no better with the sender right in the house with her, or with a drawing to be duplicated actually in her own hand or within arm's reach. Therefore, whether it is a question of thirty millimeters or thirty miles apparently does not matter to this strange process.

Coming back into our own laboratory, I might begin with a discussion of Miss Bailey, one of our most versatile subjects. Distance experiments presented no obstacles to her. As a matter of fact, she merely closed her eyes, seemed to go into a light trance, and slowly called off the symbols with a high rate of success. In the same room with the sender, in this case Miss Ownbey, in 275 trials in pure telepathy experiments, she obtained an average of 11.4 out of 25; in 450 trials in the next room and out of sight, 9.7; with 150 trials, two rooms away, an average of 12.0. The distance was between twelve and fifteen feet for each room, so that at most she was not over thirty feet away.

But what would have happened in these tests if the cards were giving off radiation such as X rays or any other short wave lengths? Close to the sender—let us say across the table at a distance of three feet—there would be radiation a hundred times as intense as there would be thirty feet away. This is to say nothing of the difficulty—indeed, the impossibility—of getting appreciable radiation from extremely short waves to pass through two walls made of building tile with certain other impediments such as bookcases between. And let us remember that skip-distance effects have not been found in such miniature waves as would have to be supposed here.

6

The still more phenomenal work of Zirkle offers support, not only of the same kind, but with much larger numbers. Miss Bailey did only about 900 trials, while Zirkle did several thousand. Zirkle's averages in the same room, one room away, and two rooms away from the sender were respectively 14.0, 14.6, and 16.0. Here again it seemed there was a little advantage in getting away from the sender instead of a pronounced falling off which would have been looked for had there been a radiation basis for this phenomenon.

It is not wise to emphasize too greatly the fact of improvement with distance, since we are not sure just how this will ultimately be regarded. It has happened with most of the subjects who have done successful distance work. I can submit only a hypothesis to explain this tendency: when the subject is in the same room with the sender or with the cards he is from long habit prone to give a certain amount of attention to them through the senses. He is sensorially aware of the presence of the cards or of the sender and he cannot adequately shut off these natural, long-used outlets of attention. When he is out of sight, out of hearing, habit turns in the opposite direction. These sensory channels are closed. There is no use trying to see or hear. He is then more prepared for that full concentration of attention upon a nonsensory attitude. Up to a certain point it might well be that the farther away the subject the better the results, although a relation proportionate to extreme distance could hardly be expected. An adverse factor might appear if the subject believed that the intervening distance was too complete a separation.

A distance of 165 miles was too much for Zirkle,

even during the period when he was doing his best work. But again one can hazard a pretty good guess to explain this failure. Zirkle, as a subject, had some difficulty in adjusting to new situations in the ESP work. For example, it took him nearly six months to adapt himself to doing clairvoyance, though he was very high in telepathy tests. How long, then, should one expect him to work at distance ESP before success would be likely to come? It did not seem worth his valuable time to try so extended an experiment. Accordingly, after a short series, the attempt was discontinued.

7

On this topic again we come back to our star subject, Pearce. As a matter of fact, our most unassailable experiments which seem to cover and meet all points of attack have been the distance tests with Pearce, conducted by Pratt and later partly witnessed by myself. In his first attempt at distance tests Pearce had been a relative failure. He did not fail entirely, although he almost did so when stationed two rooms away. His averages for all three conditions were very low for him: in the same room, 6.4; one room away, 6.1; two rooms away, 5.2.

In this work Stuart was acting as sender, and it was evident from the general results that something was wrong. Stuart can be completely exonerated from any responsibility. I am quite ready to accept the blame myself for having suggested an elaborate routine. There were to be three conditions, three distances, and a certain daily routine more or less rigidly carried out, a program widely at variance with the way we ordinarily worked with Pearce. In fact, this was the first time such a complex program had been laid down for any of our subjects, and it was the last time. When, after several thousand trials, it was clear that Pearce's work was falling off badly, the conditions were changed—not relaxed as to precautions, but rather loosened in formality and fixed routine. Thereafter when Pearce came into the laboratory for an hour or two of research he no longer knew in advance to just which tests every minute was to be given. There was an opportunity from moment to moment for him to suggest changes himself. He could say, "Let's try some DT," or "Let me go over to the next room awhile," or suggestions from the experimenter would be made. This broke the monotony and very probably contributed to his doing successful scoring.

The Pratt-Pearce tests to which I referred at the beginning of this section were made considerably later, and the distance was fixed at over 100 yards right from the start. If I remember rightly, it was Pearce who first suggested this distance, following the startling results achieved by Miss Turner. At any rate, to have done so would be quite in keeping with his personality. He liked a challenge.

The arrangements were as indicated in the illustration facing the following page. Pearce had a small cubicle in the Duke General Library. More than 100 yards away from his cubicle, on the opposite side of the library, Pratt in his research room in the Physics Building was to start the test at a time agreed upon in advance, and begin by taking the top card from an ESP pack and laying it on a book in the center of a table. After a minute of exposure this card, still face down, was laid aside and the next card was put in its place. The cards were piled up in order, waiting for the end of the run, which took twenty-five minutes. At the mid-point of each minute Pearce, with his synchronized watch, recorded in the library what he thought the symbol was on the card Pratt was handling.

After two runs had been made, Pratt turned the two packs of cards over and made a record on a slip of paper. The records were brought in a sealed envelope to me. Pearce brought his the same way. There was to be no discussion between the two until the envelopes had been delivered to me, which was done shortly after the experiment. From Pratt's window Pearce could be seen entering the library. The packs of cards were shuffled after Pearce left Pratt's room. Two packs were used each day.

As usual, Pearce started poorly. He seldom began a new condition or technique with his best scoring. On the first two days he did only three runs, obtaining 3, 8, and 5. Beginning on the third day with 9 and 10, he averaged 11.4 for the next four days that the experiment was continued. In fact, on the last day his scores were the highest. He made three runs on that day to round up the number of trials to 300, and in the three runs together, where chance score would have been 15, he obtained a total of 38.

About the only criticism that could be leveled at this work is the rather extreme supposition that Pratt and Pearce were in collusion to deceive. But even this point is covered by the fact that a little later I witnessed a three-day series under the same conditions. I stayed in the room with Pratt while the work was being carried on. I watched him shuffle the cards, I cut the pack, and I watched him record. In these 150 trials the average was 9.3. Even this short series yielded results so far above chance that, statistically speaking, the odds are over a million to one against chance's being the explanation.

Not all of Pearce's distance work was as good as this. But if he could hold up to such a level as 9.9 through 300 trials, improving as he went and going at his highest when stopped, it is enough to show that ESP does not need to fall off because of distance alone. It certainly did not fall off in his work inversely with the square of the distance, as

A PORTION OF THE MEN'S CAMPUS AT DUKE UNIVERSITY,
SHOWING THE BUILDINGS IN WHICH DISTANCE TESTS IN
ESP WERE MADE. ONE SERIES OF TESTS WAS MADE FROM
B TO C, 100 YARDS DISTANT. A SECOND WAS BETWEEN
A AND C, 250 YARDS.

light intensity or sound would do. As a matter of fact, the trials made in the same room with the cards, with Pratt as experimenter, just before and just after carrying out these tests at 100 yards, averaged only 8.2.

After deliberately stopping Pearce in the midst of his finest scoring at 100 yards, we increased the distance to 250 yards. At the same time it was necessary for Pratt himself to go to another room, and he took the cards to be used to the Duke Medical Building. Then something happened to Pearce's scoring. It was not a falling off due to distance, apparently, since in his first day's work he scored 12 and 10 per 25, which was right up to his best average. But the next day he got exactly chance. The third day he scored high again with two 10's; then the fourth day it was only a 2 and a 6, the fifth day a 5 and a 12, down again the next day to 7 and 5, and up once more to make it a perfect zigzag. But his total average for this block of work was only 6.7.

As to what started this strange alternation of high and low scoring neither Pearce nor we had or have any reliable information. In the course of twenty-two days' work, or forty-four runs, he scored zero three times. By chance alone zero would not be expected even once. On the other hand, he scored 10 or above in thirteen out of the forty-four trials. By chance, no score as high as that would be expected more than once. In three successive days he made the score 4 five times out of the six runs, the other score being a 1.

This scoring is the most peculiar that Pearce ever did. It indicates that he was almost alternately successful and unsuccessful, but when he was at his best he did quite as well as, in fact better than, when he was in the same room with the cards. When he was having a poor day he did worse than chance. After performing in this curious way at the longer distance, Pratt moved back to the Physics Building for another 300 trials to ascertain if the change had been in Pearce or in the conditions. The result was an average of 7.2, only a little above the average of 6.7 which had been obtained just before at the longer distance. It thus appeared that the change had been in Pearce, and this further supports the internal evidence that it was not increased distance that had led to the up-and-down scoring.

Naturally we wanted still greater distance between Pearce and the cards. The time did not seem appropriate to try it in view of Pearce's decline on the latest trials at 100 yards. But in this work there is always a risk, so we took a chance. The next step involved a distance of two miles, and things went wrong from the start. The room arranged for was not open when it should have been and for several days there was frustration in the physical details of the experiment. After things were finally straightened out, there was no appreciable success.

Seeing that Pearce had rather lost his spirit in the matter, we gave up the project.

An attempt was then made in another direction: sending Pearce out in my car to different points in the country, he was asked to record calls at different distances as registered on the speedometer. No success came in the few days of trial made with this, and largely because Pearce was not hopeful, we did not push him further. Theoretically there was little that could be added on the point on which we were then concentrating, and the finer ramifications of ESP at a distance will have to be worked out when facilities are more freely at our disposal and the control of conditions more satisfactory.

There remains only the unique but brief series of Miss Turner and her phenomenal long-distance series of 200 trials. Enough has already been said about this 250-mile distant experiment in ESP. But nothing has been offered by anyone to explain it away, unless conceivably there was some collusion between Miss Ownbey, my trusted experimental assistant for several years, and Miss Turner, whose reputation, too, is beyond reproach. Miss Turner had never before made a score of 19, which was what she got on the first day's run. Can one imagine a wave hypothesis applying to these results? Can Miss Ownbey in Durham have been so powerful a "broadcasting station" that 250 miles would only improve the clarity of her reception?

8

For that matter, on any wave theory the percipient, or receiver, would presumably have to be
screening out radiations from the brains of all the
rest of the inhabited globe, especially if distance
makes no appreciable difference. If 250 miles is
only a good start, then from all sides impressions
would be coming in upon the poor, defenseless
subject's "receiving station," impressions which
would presumably contain some circles and stars
and plus signs or at least would contain a great
deal of static. What remarkable selection one
would have to attribute to any hypothetical waves,
even if there were no further difficulties to be considered!

From all the facts, then, singly or jointly considered, there is nothing to favor a wave theory
except the fact that it is ready at hand, and on a
number of points it would be excluded by the
nature of the evidence.

But if not waves, then what? When waves are
ruled out are all the known energies eliminated?
Perhaps it would be perilous to say anything definite in view of the present state of flux in the field
of physics. As a matter of fact, we do not find in
our discussions with physicists that they are ready
to offer any physical hypotheses beyond the range
of the analogies of known wave mechanics.

9

But still there is a strong disposition, which I myself share, to try to regard these phenomena of ESP as somehow within the pale of energy causation, energetic in the sense that something occurs which in the end achieves work, brings about change, even though as yet the number of work units which are achieved in a given trial or run has not actually been studied. Certainly, when Miss Turner is so guided by Miss Ownbey 250 miles away that she is led to put down a certain set of symbols, 19 of them correct, there is causation of the one person's set of results by the other's action as an agent, just as clearly as if the percipient had been guided by an electrical circuit. We need not understand the method of causation to recognize that this is a fact. And if Miss Ownbey has led Miss Turner to do work, in the physicist's sense of the word, there must have been, according to present conceptions of the definition of energy, an energetic connection. Yet if the inverse square law, which holds that energy decreases as the square of the distance, and other criteria of mechanics limit the mechanical energetics ESP, we have, curiously enough, come round by what we regard as a strictly evidential and experimental route to just the position that the man behind so much of this ESP research, Professor McDougall, has long maintained on other grounds: that in mental processes a nonmechanical and, as he calls it, teleological but not mystical mode of causation is in operation. Now, all that these formidable terms mean in the last analysis is that something peculiarly purposive and personal is going on in the activity of the mind and that this is something over and above the laws of mechanics as we know them.

The thing to remember about physics is that, however well developed it seems in comparison with the other sciences, it has scarcely touched the problems of the working of the simplest protoplasm. Physics has not yet approached the threshold of the nature of life. In spite of the brilliance of recent researches, the principal physics of the nervous system is still a great mystery. A mere sensation, the simplest element of mind—if we can thus arbitrarily speak of it—is too far beyond the present frontiers of physics for us even to conjecture how great the gap may be. And the physics of sensation is probably relatively simple, relatively easy in contrast to the physics of higher mental processes.

What physics will be like when it advances through these fields of untouched problems we can at this time have scarcely the faintest notion. What it may be prepared ultimately to include in its scope it would be foolish to conjecture. It is well to be open to the possibility that expanding physics may sometime be prepared to deal with the phenomenon of ESP even though it seems at present to have none but the remotest intercourse with it.

The concept of a nonmechanical energy or a nonmechanical physics which might include the phenomena of mind is little more than a logical category. If it serves to indicate an open-mindedness to the possibility of thus unifying what we know from one field with what we have known from others, we may put it down as one of the possibilities; but put down alongside that possibility the statement that a physics or energetics which embraced ESP and other related mental processes would be so free from the limitations of the present scope of mechanics that those who dread too close an alliance between mind and mechanics need have no concern over such a contiguity.

10

These people who have long ago been led to discard a wave theory of ESP and who have searched in all logical quarters for another way to explain it, for some other hypothesis, have not had much success. What they have had to do is to suppose cosmic reservoirs or absolutes of some kind which contain all knowledge of everything there is and ever will be. They must also suppose that the mind of man can, as it were, telephone in to these great central sources of information and draw at liberty upon them. The "cosmic consciousness" or any other great suppositional source of information, or even the extreme view that possibly spirits of the dead co-operate as messengers, signaling from a higher point of vantage, do not help in the solution of the problem of extra-sensory perception. Without attempting to rule them out of consideration, one need only say that they still leave us with the same old problem on our hands: How does ESP occur?

Even if a friendly incorporeal personality or spirit were to look at the cards on Pratt's table and rush instantaneously to Pearce in the library in the Duke Physics Building with the knowledge, guiding his hand to put it down on paper, how could we, then, account for Pearce's knowing that symbol before he put it down on paper? Only by an assumption of telepathy from the incorporeal spirit to Pearce. And how account for the supposed spirit's getting knowledge of the symbol from the card without eyes, without senses? Extra-sensory perception? Or suppose one does tap the "cosmic reservoir." It would have to be done extra-sensorially, since we possess no senses which can look into such an unseen world of mysteries. Again, extra-sensory perception! What is the use, then, of these more elaborate hypotheses? The law of parsimony, which declares that other things being equal the simplest explanation is the best one, rules them out until they become a factual necessity. To say the least, that time is not here yet.

But a good, healthy science does not need to have all its problems solved at one moment. Only hasty speculators cannot face waiting and searching until the facts themselves give the right answer. In the fullness of time—plus a great deal of hard work—it seems likely that hypotheses in plenty will rise out of the very experiments set up to yield the facts. Until that time we must admit that we do not have any intelligent hypothesis of the fundamental nature of ESP. There is ahead of us the adventure of finding out.

CHAPTER XIII

Who Has Extra-Sensory Perception?

Even if we cannot explain exactly what ESP is, what energy is uses, or how it fits into the world of sense and mechanics, there are other interesting things about it, and some of them can be answered fairly definitely. For example, how widespread is the ESP ability among people in general? In an earlier chapter I referred to the estimate, made at Duke some years ago, of one in five as about the proportion of subjects who could demonstrate extra-sensory perceptivity with our card tests. Since that time the various searches for good subjects in other colleges and universities has confirmed this rough average. Does this mean that the four who do not show significant scores are without the ESP faculty? At present I am inclined to believe that this is not necessarily the case. There are fairly reliable indications that anyone in good health and free from worry, fatigue, or other limiting causes may do significant work *if he can be interested and can be persuaded to co-operate fully and try patiently.* Securing this attitude is partly the responsibility of the investigator, and better techniques for doing so may perhaps be worked out later.

Not much has been said so far in this book about what kinds of people are most likely to display special aptitude for ESP. Points like this are not among the best established aspects of our work; on the other hand, they are not so important as to require a high degree of experimental verification. Any public discussion of the whole subject generally gets round to the problem of personality and extra-sensory capacity sooner or later. Are women more often gifted than men? Does age have anything to do with the case? Are there any known factors of race, color, or physical condition which seem to affect the occurrence of ESP? There is no reason why a few suggested answers to these questions may not be given here, with the replies based in part on work that is to be published in full later on.

2

It is clear that age is not a limiting factor. Among the subjects who got significant results have been people ranging in age from four to sixty. The older people are on the whole more steady, while the interest in scoring ability on the part of children is relatively short-lived. There does not seem to be any correlation of ability with age, but some age groups are more suitable to work with, for secondary reasons. It is easier to secure the co-operation of young people because their time is freer and they demand less rational explanation to justify their entering into the tests. This point is easiest of all, of course, with children; but the problem of maintaining interest is the difficulty in their case. Some of the best projects at the present time are being conducted with children, and one perfect score (that is, a run of 25 successive hits) was made by a child of twelve. But in general the most satisfactory work is still being done with college students, who have served as subjects in practically all the university studies before and since the Duke experiments began.

There does not seem to be any superiority of women over men in this regard; we have had about equal success with both sexes. The results of several series give a reasonably strong impression that in telepathy there is an added advantage in having sender and receiver of opposite sexes. This may be due to that touch of added entertainment which we customarily find in that particular social situation. The problem of racial comparisons has not yet been adequately explored.

As to intelligence, our subjects have ranged from Duke's most capable students down to approximately average students. So far none has been below average. In exploring for subjects, persons with subaverage intelligence have not yet been particularly sought out, but in the study of school children made by Miss Bond, already referred to,

COMPETITIVE SCREENED OPEN MATCHING TEST. CHIL-
DREN TAKE THE TEST AS A GAME.

her own retarded pupils of the fourth and fifth grades were used as subjects. There were twenty of them classified at various levels of retardation. No significant relation was found between intelligence and level of scoring ability, nor has anything so far suggested any correlation of ESP ability with the general level of intelligence as judged by scholastic work. Clearly, factors other than intelligence are concerned.

3

Does the ESP ability grow greater with learning or practice, after the subject has once accustomed himself to the technique of a particular test? Apparently not. The fact that there has been no perceptible "learning curve" or increase of proficiency in the performance of the subjects with whom we have worked makes it unlikely that any correlation will later be found with general learning ability. Cooper got one of his best scores during the first 50 trials he was ever given. Stuart's first 500 were the best he did out of 10,000 trials. Pearce rose to his best level during the first hundred; Linzmayer did likewise. And so it goes.

For some time Stuart attempted to develop the view that there was some connection between artistic interest and ESP ability. He himself is artistically gifted and so are the other good subjects. A few of the remainder, however, have only such artistic appreciation as involves enjoying music or appreciating some other form of art. The total number of subjects we have worked with is still too small to permit any reliable correlation, and there are some marked exceptions.

The question whether the blind are especially competent ESP subjects has often been asked. A preliminary study of this point has at last been made, with Miss Margaret Pegram and Miss Margaret Price, of the Duke laboratory, in charge. They worked largely with the blind boys and men from a school not far from the university. The results of their tests certainly show a more-than-average likelihood of a blind person's possessing ESP ability. Of the total number of blind persons they tested, between a third and a half showed significant results. The conditions of the investigation were excellent, and it looks, at least superficially, as if blind people may show some compensating superiority in this nonsensory mode of perception.

But there are other possibilities to account for the higher scores made by the blind, and the experimenters themselves wisely refrain from taking any position except a noncommittal one. The blind subjects may simply have been more hopeful, or more interested, and so proved better subjects on the score of attitude rather than through the development of a greater capacity for ESP.

Little, if anything, then, can be said that will characterize the successful ESP subject as different

in mind or personality from those who do not succeed. Those traits which seem at present to give an
indication of the sort of people who will make
promising subjects would really characterize only
the sort of person who is most likely to have atti-
tudes of mind favorable to trying out the tests.
In other words, we might say such-and-such a
person will be likely to enter into the experiments
wholeheartedly or will have no inhibitions about
it. About the only reliable predisposing characteristic that may be used with any assurance—and it
should be used with considerable reservation—is a
genuine enthusiasm for being tested for the sake of
the test itself, as a game or performance, and it
is hard to pick out people on this basis or to find
anything in the known process of the mind with
which this observation can be calculated. But this
is not to say that it cannot eventually be done.

4

There is, however, one particular sort of human
being to whom it is worth paying special attention
in this discussion. In all ages and in all times there
have been certain persons who have been believed
to possess unusual powers. In many cases these
powers seem to have been at least partly extra-
sensory perceptive, either clairvoyant or telepathic
or both. Such uncommonly endowed men and
women have been variously known as soothsayers,

sybils, witches, pythonesses, priests, priestesses, and oracles; in modern times they are referred to generally as mediums, clairvoyants, or fortunetellers. The word "medium" is, of course, taken from the vocabulary of spiritualism and implies the hypothesis that the special powers in question come from the spirits of the dead. In short, mediums are believed to intermediate between their clients and these spirits.

Whatever may be the reader's beliefs about spiritualism and mediums, certainly he will agree that the opportunity to test a professionally successful medium for ESP was much to be desired. Such a chance came our way when Mrs. Eileen Garrett, the British medium, visited this country in the spring of 1934. Mrs. Garrett had already achieved an international reputation among the psychical research societies.

There was at least one astonishing story of her powers which rests upon the authority of a well-known psychiatrist on the Pacific coast. An experiment in telepathy was arranged between Mrs. Garrett, who was in California at the time, and a certain doctor in the remote island of Iceland, a place in the neighborhood of 4,400 miles away. At a given moment Mrs. Garrett was to attempt to get in telepathic communication with this man and report what he was doing. She did so, and the subsequent checkup revealed, according to report, that not only had she described correctly various smaller circumstances, but she had even been able to report that he was injured, a fact unknown in California. This story, so reminiscent of the ancient tale of the test which King Croesus of Lydia imposed upon various oracles in his search for a reliable one, whetted our desire to test Mrs. Garrett under laboratory conditions, and her willingness to let us test her made it appear that she would make an ideal subject.

Our first interest, of course, was to obtain a measure of her ability as a subject in our ordinary card-calling and telepathic tests. It was soon obvious that Mrs. Garrett did not enjoy the card tests, and I learned indirectly that she disliked them vigorously from the beginning, protesting that they were, for her, an overmechanization of the extra-sensory process. She was used to doing clairvoyant work in personal relations with people and not with mere routine handling of packs of cards. This is not an unreasonable difference, and her attitude was quite understandable although it was unusual among the subjects tested.

At any rate, while Mrs. Garrett began at once to score well on the telepathic tests and did so with different senders, both in the same room and one or two rooms away, she did not do well with the card-calling tests; and it was only after several days' work that she rose to an average per day that became significant of her actual clairvoyant capacity. Taken as a whole, her work in clairvoyance was significant, but lower than that of many of our own subjects. Her telepathic work, on the contrary, was in a class with that of our very best subjects. In fairness to Mrs. Garrett, as well as to my own view of the close relationship between clairvoyance and telepathy, the fact of her dislike for the card-calling technique is a plausible explanation for her lower results in clairvoyance.

For many readers the most interesting aspect of the work with Mrs. Garrett will be that which was done in trance. Spiritists believe that in the trance state of mediums a change of personality occurs. The new personality speaks in a different voice from the medium's own, displays other differences of personality, and claims to know facts of which the medium is personally ignorant. In Mrs. Garrett's case the most frequent trance personality is one describing himself as the spirit of an ancient Arab by the name of Uvani. Uvani claims Mrs. Garrett as his instrument; he states that he himself does not possess clairvoyant or telepathic power, but that when he takes part in the tests it is the instrument whose power he uses. I cannot understand how, were he a spirit, Uvani could get along without these extra-sensory modes of perception, since presumably senses are a part of the body which he left on the sands of Arabia centuries ago. But this is beside the point.

The interesting fact is that the Uvani personality, whatever his relation with the Mrs. Garrett personality, averaged close to the results obtained by Mrs. Garrett in the waking state. The most remarkable point is that he, too, showed the high telepathic and the low clairvoyant capacity which she did; and this is the only work in which we have had a marked difference in that direction. Add to this the fact that both telepathy and clairvoyance curves for Mrs. Garrett showed first a steady rise and then a steady drop during the three weeks of investigation. Further, when the trance tests began, they ran through approximately similar rates of decline, both in telepathy and in clairvoyance. Altogether, then, the results indicated a close similarity between the tests in trance and the tests in the waking state. Uvani would seem to be right: the gifts are the gifts of the medium, whatever Uvani himself may be.

Does this difference between telepathy and clairvoyance constitute an exception to my view of the essentially fundamental relationship between these two? Probably not. Rather, in the fact that both waking and trance conditions showed closely parallel results, it seems to furnish some further confirmation of the view that the two powers are related. Here were two states of personality in which similar conditions brought about similar changes in both telepathy and clairvoyance simultaneously. Something was operating to diminish the subject's clairvoyance or else increase her telepathy, but this could well happen in accord-

ance with the view that telepathy and clairvoyance
are basically rooted in the same process.

Altogether, the work with Mrs. Garrett was
among the most interesting we have done. Her
averages, omitting a final week during which she
was manifestly ill, were about 10.1 for telepathy
in the waking state and 9.1 in trance. The more
than 8,000 trials with clairvoyance averaged only
5.7 in the waking state and 5.6 in trance. But even
so, with such a large number, they were very significant. During the high point in her curve, for
a three-day period she rose to an average of 6.3 in
clairvoyance in 3,500 runs and to 13.4 in telepathy.

5

But we did not test Mrs. Garrett solely by the
routine procedures of the laboratory. In fairness
to her own professional method we thought it
proper to test her under her own conditions. Accordingly, a series of sittings, as they are called,
was arranged whereby persons unknown to her
could be brought to the laboratory under carefully
guarded conditions, with a view to finding out
whether information could be given them that
could not have been obtained by Mrs. Garrett by
the normal methods of sense or of reason. To exclude the senses, the subject was brought into the
room only after the medium was put into trance.
The subject was then seated behind her and was

asked to remain silent throughout the sitting and to leave before the medium awoke from trance, in case there were to be other sittings for the same visitor. Stenographic records were taken of all that the medium said. During a second series even greater precautions were taken to make sure that the medium had no sensory contact with the visiting subject. In this series the sitter was kept in an adjoining room with a closed door between.

One of the objectives in these experiments was to secure records of the medium's remarks without the visitor's hearing what she said. Records made under these conditions, and of all the sittings together could be shown to the various sitters without any one of them knowing which particular record contained the medium's comments intended for him. His judgment could be secured upon all of them and would be relatively free from bias or, if bias was shown, it would be equally great for all the sittings, and the danger thus would be eliminated.

A method of evaluation for this sort of work with mediums has been devised by two Englishmen, H. F. Saltmarsh and S. G. Soal. It makes possible a mathematical expression of relative success or failure with fair precision, or at least on the side of safety. Dr. Pratt, who was in charge of this project and who has since published a written record of it, prepared a long questionnaire based on the records of Mrs. Garrett's sittings. This questionnaire was submitted to all the sitters and each one answered all the points listed, not only his own but those for all the others. From these answers a value was computed for each sitting. In these mediumistic records, extra-sensorially obtained knowledge was manifest in connection with several visiting subjects. Also, the work as a whole passed the mathematical criterion of extra-chance results.

It must be pointed out, however, that, though Mrs. Garrett acquitted herself well in all these activities, the simple routine tests for telepathy and clairvoyance showed with greater economy of energy and much more clarity her capacities for extra-sensory perception.

Whether there is something beyond these natural capacities for extra-sensory perception, whether there is something more working in the Uvani personality in trance, as he insists, we have no way of knowing and as yet no way of finding out with any degree of assurance. There is no need on this occasion even to express a leaning. For that problem of parapsychology needs a vast preparation and a secure foundation for long research.

CHAPTER XIV

The Mailbag

WHEN THE FIRST TECHNICAL REPORT ON THE Duke experiments to be presented in book form —*Extra-Sensory Perception*—appeared in 1934, one reviewer, after discussing the book itself, ended his article by saying, "I foresee for Professor Rhine a large increase in his mail." He was right. There have been letters, thousands of them, from every sort of place and person from the moment when something of what we were doing became publicly known. A representative sample of our mailbag reveals what meaning has been given to our researches by the general public and what kind of suggestions and questions the work has brought forth.

Almost every letter that came into the office has been acknowledged and, if possible, answered. Most of this mail is interesting from one point of view or another. Much of it has been helpful, and some of it extraordinarily so. Through this correspondence, for one thing, a network of co-workers over the country has been established, and through their collaboration our capacity for research has been greatly increased. Something of the extent of this interested co-operation was indicated in a previous chapter.

2

First for some of the less profitable but interesting letters. There is no doubt that through working with the mysteries of telepathy and clairvoyance we have won recognition from all the brotherhood which William James terms the "lunatic fringe" of humanity. (I would not use so harsh a term myself.)

In spite of years of inquiry with some phase or other of this subject, I had never dreamed there were so many brands and branches of the "occult sciences" as there really are in practice in this country. How many strange cults and odd philosophies seem to be established and flourishing, how many imposing titles that imply transcendent powers of mind and body, how many opportunities for the development of one's hidden capacities! The laboratory must have come into contact with every one of them by this time.

Our answer to these usually sincere "seekers-after-truth" is that they and we do not speak the same language, that while we, too, are seeking after truth we are limited to a strict method and procedure and that our only feeling of safety rests in adhering closely to that discipline, regardless of temptations to follow short-cut paths that may

be advertised to us. Furthermore, none of us at
Duke can afford to attach ourselves to groups who
do not use such a method, because we wish to carry
with us a substantial body of scientific men who
can see what we see in our observation and experiments and who can help to interpret these results.
Finally, unless our correspondents are willing to
adopt the rigid experimental and quantitative
treatment, there can be no degree of co-operation.
As a rule, that reply ends the matter.

Sometimes these holders of the key to mystery
want to come for a personal interview, to explain
"the real science, the oldest of them all"—astrol-
ogy, of course—and tell us what wonderful work
is being done through its aid. Or, sometimes we
get a letter from a pyramidologist, with a key to
the prophetic mysteries of the pyramids, who sees
how open-minded we are and feels that we must
be kindred spirits. Now and again the correspondent is someone who has traveled far and seen many
strange mysteries, from Tibet to Timbuktu, from
Lily Dale to Hollywood. Some of them even get
as far as Durham, plump themselves down in my
office, and want to help me experiment, because
they have seen things such as I have never dreamed
of seeing. There is the woman who has seen them
with her own eyes. She has acquired disciplines that
would make my experiments seem trifling. Twenty
per cent above chance? A hundred per cent right

232   NEW FRONTIERS OF THE MIND

is *her* average! Of course, there is always a theoretical background. "The lotus has opened" or she
has been initiated by special contact with an orien-
tal priest into mysteries beyond my comprehen-
sion. Over and over I go through my standard
routine explanation.

First, I do appreciate—or try to—such interest
and sincerity. But, in science as in religion, one
may say, "By their fruits ye shall know them."

"If you have some special power, we will be
interested to have you show it to us in any way
that will be convincing to us and other students
of science. You will not even need to tell us how
you do it to get us interested. But please *do it first!*
Please take some reliable test method. You are welcome to use the tests which we will give you, or
if you can devise better ones, more suited to your
purpose, we shall be glad to go over them and see
your results. If you find you can do the things
you say you can, under test conditions, with yourself or with others, we'll go a long way to study
with you and help you bring your work before
a scientific audience. Whether you use the 'oldest
of the sciences' or the pyramids or Yoga or the
lines of the palm matters not in the least, if you
can produce good, clear-cut results that permit of
only one interpretation, that of perception without sensory means. If you cannot, you are outside our field of study. Until you prove your

powers objectively, we haven't much in common or at least we do not know that we have."

At that point I look anxiously at my watch or at the door or at the mail from other inquirers which I have not yet been able to read. Sometimes that works. Not always. . . .

Yet I must not leave the impression that we are unsympathetic to these people. All we are unsympathetic to is the way they are floundering about without a line, a method, to pull them ashore. In my judgment they represent intelligent humanity of a prescientific era. Many of them are fine, aspiring souls trying to find a better explanation of man and a better code of action for his conduct. The fact that I have the instrument of scientific method to use and am that much more fortunate makes me want to find for them such truth as there may be, though they may be all too ready to accept it, even uncritically.

Even when one of us is called in to investigate a blindfolded boy trickster, a theatrical "telepathy" performer, or a fraudulent medium, we do not try to disillusion their clients or victims by a public statement. The task of research is to find what is true. The exposure of fraud is a practical social problem not in our line. There are those who will censure us for this stand. But it is, I think, highly defensible both on practical and on aesthetic grounds. Besides, we do not want to waste precious time wrangling with the ever-present sponsors and defenders of every fake. I have been all through that once and am convinced that in general it is a bad policy.

3

A surprisingly large number of letters have almost the same general wording and always move me to more pity than do any other communications we receive. The writer will explain that he or she has been the victim of telepathy, of telepathic approaches from someone, usually specified more or less clearly. Someone, these letters say, is trying to force his or her attentions upon the sufferer, persecuting him. Commonly there will be an explanation of the reasons for this persecution. The appeal is made to us for some way of shielding the victim from these approaches.

What can we do for such people beyond pitying them? We usually explain that they need have no fear of telepathy's being so used, that it is weak enough at best, and that we have no evidence whatever of the possibility of its being employed in any harmful way. As gently as we can we suggest that worries of this kind can often be helped by talking with a person who understands the mind, and if there is a doctor near by whose specialty is the field of mental problems he should be consulted.

Such people are the last, I suspect, actually to

have genuine telepathic experiences. Certainly the few who have been tested in mental hospitals—people who suffer from delusions of persecution through the medium of telepathy—have not shown the capacity at all. For these estimates I am indebted to two friends, both on the staffs of mental hospitals.

4

Another interesting group of correspondents from whom we hear occasionally are those who regard themselves as "potentially psychic," as they say, and wish to develop their powers. Sooner or later, probably, such people get into contact with persons who are only too eager to help them develop their powers—in so many lessons at so much per lesson. But from us they receive at most a few instructions in ESP technique and perhaps a pack of cards, and that much only if they seem able to follow the instructions or to appreciate what the results might mean.

Our mail is seldom without calls for practical help, the writers apparently believing that anyone working in such a field must have around him a great many clairvoyant subjects who can, for example, tell the writer where he has mislaid an important document, whether he is going to be given the appointment for which he has applied, or identify the person who is suspected of persecuting the writer.

By far the largest part of our "psychic" mail deals with the mere relation of personal experiences. "I read about your work in such-and-such magazine. I thought you would be interested in an experience I once had," and the stories follow: They come from all over the country in almost every mail. The story usually bears directly upon our work in that the capacities for which we are testing would have to be assumed to explain the occurrence.

Such letters are always acknowledged and commented upon so far as may be possible. The writers are in almost all cases deeply impressed by the experiences and write with a ring of sincerity that one feels is beyond question. It is not difficult to recognize from the first few lines the kind of story any particular one is going to be, and we can almost always predict the outcome. Familiarity with these experiences is worth while and, though it is not humanly possible for one person to read all of them carefully, I should not want these writers to discontinue sending in their experiences. And when a polite inquiry is submitted as to whether we like to have such instances sent to us, we always answer in the affirmative.

Someday perhaps our files of this sort of material will be utilized in some research of a classificatory or analytical nature. In the meantime they serve to keep us here in the laboratory alive to the vivid actual experiences of people outside our walls, experiences which seem to be related to the

principles for which we are making tests. Perhaps
they will keep us from becoming narrow in our
concept of the problems. Perhaps in these experiences may come suggestions as to what to try to
find. We cannot, of course, accept them as evidence, although to say this is not to cast doubt
upon the veracity of the writers in any case. These
letters comprise a great bulk of suggestive material.

5

Some of our best suggestions for further work
have come through the mail. Indeed, some able
and experienced correspondents have given us their
attention and the benefit of their judgment unsparingly. We have in our files dozens of good ideas
or suggestions waiting for the time when we can
secure a laboratory staff adequate to follow them
up. These suggestions would involve too much detailed explanation and technical discussion to outline here. But there are certain general questions
that come repeatedly, and we shall doubtless receive these very same questions by the dozen from
readers of this book if they are not covered here.

"Why do you not vary your technique?" is one of
these common questions. It would be more interesting, the writer continues, if we were to use other
objects besides cards and not adhere through thousands of trials to our monotonous pluses, circles,
waves, and so forth. This must be very uninterest-

ing to the subject, they say, whereas if we were to
use photographs, objects, drawings, or material rich
in emotional association the subject would do much
better because of his greater interest.

Our usual reply is that variety in the test material would have many points in its favor and that
certain experiments will eventually be made to
analyze its effect. Earlier experimenters did vary
their material. But we have in mind certain objections that would not be met in this way. We want
to find out the nature of this process, the conditions under which it succeeds, and so on. The research could furnish effective comparisons only, in
the main, by adhering to the same material. As a
matter of fact, we do make certain departures,
but only for specific ends.

Furthermore, it is not the object itself that
creates interest in the tests; it is the goal the subject has in calling the object, and our subjects do
become very much interested in calling the cards,
so much so that one of them working alone called
185,000, with in some cases as many as 5,000 in
one day. The cards themselves are not objects of
interest any more than the letters and figures on
a ten-dollar bill are themselves the objects of interest. The symbols, as the figures, merely serve a
purpose. It is the purpose that we are interested in.
The subject calls the cards because he wants to
make a score. It might only distract him if there
were faces of movie stars or baseball players on

the cards. That is something to be investigated by
later experiment.

Finally, this rigid adherence to our simple test
materials cannot be fully justified without a complete account of our whole research program,
which is out of the question in a letter. In fact, it
is difficult to make it adequately clear even in an
entire book. But those who are close to the work
itself do not in general urge us to any appreciable
departure from our five forms.

Along with this question of variety in the cards
comes one closely associated: "Can anything but
your symbols be transmitted? What about emo-
tions? Can a person reliably tell when someone is
staring at him? Can anyone be forced to do something through telepathic influence by another?"
To such questions, which are usually good ones
in a way, the answer has to be: "These are somewhat aside from the main trend of our present
research. We cannot cut too wide a swath. These
questions should be answered in a lateral expan-
sion of our research which we hope someday to
be able to secure by increasing our resources."
Wherever there appears to be any likelihood that
the writer himself is capable of competent investigation we urge that he undertake a study himself,
at least of preliminary character. It must not be
thought that we expect to get full-fledged scientific developments from everybody to whom we
send a pack of cards or whom we urge to investi-

gate. Investigation along such simple lines as these does no one any harm, is commonly of good entertainment value, and is the best way of answering many questions, as well as, wherever it is possible, developing powers of observation. From such amateur beginners in investigation mature scientists may develop in this work as they have done in the past in astronomy, geology, radio-physics, and other fields of interest.

6

Among the letters are many suggesting tricks we might play on the subject. The writers apparently believe this to be the best way to find out what is really going on in the subject's mind. One of the tricks most often suggested is that of slipping in a blank deck of cards without the subject's knowledge; or substituting an altered deck, putting in ten circles, say, and leaving out all the stars. Some of these correspondents suggest that a stacked deck be used, with all the symbols of one kind grouped together. Such suggestions are usually well meant, even though they are not, for different reasons, useful in our studies. In the first place, we have from the beginning followed the principle of not attempting to deceive the subject. To do so might well undermine his confidence, and the whole procedure requires confidence and the best of personal relations. When it is argued that

of course the subject need not be told, the answer
is that this is begging the question. If the subject
possesses ESP capacity he may very well catch on
to what we were doing without being told or
he might be affected by realizing that something
is wrong without knowing exactly what it is. We
cannot afford to take a chance of this kind.

Furthermore, there is no need to do so. The basic
purpose of these suggestions is to find out whether
the subject is really doing ESP or whether the results are merely chance coincidence. To such writers we submit that, if a subject's calling a pack of
25 cards correctly is not sufficient evidence, recognizing that a blank pack was blank would certainly not be, and no one would be convinced by
such a case. If the subject were told that there
might be a blank pack of cards, or that one out
of every two decks might be blank, then the
chances on these would simply be 1 in 2 and success or failure would mean no more than succeeding or failing in calling circles or pluses.

Altering the deck or stacking the deck again
would simply be to test clairvoyance in a slightly
different way. But no one has shown that this way
would be in any respect superior. Once or twice,
it is true, accidentally stacked cards have been used.
Two new packs were once picked up and called
without the experimenter's knowing that the cards
had not been shuffled and the original grouping
broken up. The particular subject made good

scores on these stacked decks—as good as he had been making on the usual shuffled ones. But what was proved by that? Nothing, so far as we can see.

But even when we disagree with a suggestion we appreciate the spirit in which it is offered. It makes no difference if the suggestion be made in a harshly critical way. Entirely apart from considerations of courtesy, we have to remember that if we are to be saved from error we need criticism even more than we need encouragement.

7

On another question we have a good many letters, some pointing in one direction and some in the other. They are on a problem that does have two good sides. One group urges us to have our subjects go slow and concentrate on images, try to develop introspection, and find out in that way what ESP is all about. The group on the other side takes the view that we would do much better to speed up the process, enabling and encouraging the subject to go at his best gait in order, the argument goes, to get in as many hits as he possibly can when he is having a lucky streak or a favorable mood. The first side points to Bender's work, reviewed in an earlier chapter, and his fruitful study of images and introspective reports. Psychologists, in particular, urge this way of proceeding. From the very beginning, indeed, they have been after us for more introspective data. The other group wants us to develop the performance and concentrate on getting better scores, and some of them suggest that motorizing and automatizing the response will conduce favorably to that end after the manner of Tyrrell's machine which has been described.

To both views we say, of course, that we want to do just what each urges. Both hold an excellent point of view and there is no reason why work on both should not be promoted as actively as possible. All of us at our laboratory being, however, either active college teachers or graduate students, we find it impossible to do everything we would like to do, at least as things are at present. The fact that many such suggestions lie untried from year to year may seem discouraging to those correspondents who do not have the dozens of other suggestions and the whole research plan in mind.

We recently received a letter from an eminent English professor of the physical sciences—with those really distinguishing initials, F.R.S., Fellow of the Royal Society, after his name—who had earlier written very emphatically telling us just what we should do in order to make our work sound. A year went by after the first letter and a paper came out from this laboratory in published form; it had been written about two years earlier but held up in press. The professor read it. He saw no mention of his suggestion. He wrote us in sharp tones to the effect that he could only conclude that we had tried out his suggestions and, having failed to secure good results with them, had omitted the whole thing.

Another professor of one of the physical sciences in an American college wrote recently that he, too, had had a similar attitude. But, having written me his criticism, he set to work to try his hand at the tests themselves. His lowest score was above 5 and his highest 18, with an average above 10. He then wrote that he had, in spite of his difficulty, changed his mind. Naturally we like that kind of letter better than the first professor's. But they all add to the zest of our explorations.

8

One of the most persistent lines of suggestion that we get from physicists, engineers, and those of like mind urges us to try setting up certain physical barriers — substances that bar out waves and energies of various kinds. These students of physical science want to get at the matter by a series of elimination tests. Usually they have made out an orderly, systematic plan of attack. It is a pleasure to read them; one sees the working of first-rate intellects.

In our replies to this kind of suggestion we ask, first, "What is the object of screening?" Invariably the answer is, "To eliminate radiation." The waves to be eliminated are, of course, electromagnetic. Usually the final step proposed by these writers includes an electric circuit screen which will intercept all radiation. We then set to work to summarize the evidence against wave theories, because, we explain, if we have adequate evidence to determine the conclusion of this research beforehand, it will save an enormous amount of time and expense to avoid having to do it. Our letters on this topic often end: "However, it would be advisable for someone to try just this approach. Are you in a position to do so? We are hoping, of course, that this will eventually be done, but it has not been to date." Whether our arguments dissuade the writers from doing the work, or whether they would not have done it in any case, we do not know. Nevertheless, I really do hope there is someone who will not be convinced without an actual research and will someday carry out this series of explorations. We may find something that was not anticipated, and in any case it will give us a good answer to that oft-repeated question. We should regret, however, anything that would discourage suggestions coming from these inventive, open minds which have been writing us from physical laboratories, research laboratories, industrial companies, and other places.

Now and again we receive requests worded something like this: "Could you arrange a demonstration of your good subjects? I could get up a committee of scientists to come down and witness them

at work." Or "Could you not arrange to have one
of your good subjects work with a one-way screen
and invite a number of scientists, whom I should
like to specify, to appear behind the screen and witness them perform? The testimony of these scientists would be of great value to your work if the
results justified their testimony." Or "Could you
send one or two of your best subjects up to this
university for demonstration purposes over some
week end?"

In answer to such questions we have to explain
that the performance of these subjects is for them
a delicate matter. "Would you expect, if we had
a young poet here, that we could send him up to
your university to write some poems for you while
your committee sat staring fixedly at him to see that
he did not slip them from one of his pockets? Many
students are unable to do themselves justice in examinations in which they are supervised by staring
professors, even in cases where all they need to do
is simply to recall what they have memorized. The
process of ESP is apparently even more easily interfered with than one like memory, and we have to
grant it its own conditions if we want to find it
operating." So we answer and hope the explanation
is sufficient. But it is dangerous to ask for any special
terms or concessions. The critic is too prone to say,
"Aha, alibi!"

We often add, too, that science has never been
advanced by the committee method. Mesmer had

OPEN MATCHING

his committees, with our own broad-minded Benjamin Franklin on one of them at that, but they served only to drive him into exile. One could not ask a larger committee than the Royal Society which had earlier sat in judgment on Franklin's electricity experiments. The fact that it at one time rejected his work and refused him membership had little to do with the ultimate merit of the case. How many good men have been rejected and mistreated by the French Academy, that great committee of France's most learned and eminent men?

No, indeed, the history of science advises us to beware of research by committee. Our plan for the advancement of the subject has been, rather, to encourage young open-minded men to take up the task of finding out for themselves. One good piece of work of a confirmatory nature done in another laboratory is worth more to the scientific public than the mere testimony of a committee of the most eminent scientists at large.

9

Now and then the mail brings us questions about the bearing of our work upon the immortality of the soul, the survival of personality. Such questions have often come from people who give a recent bereavement as their reason for asking. I wish with all my heart that we could give a scientific reply to these letters, that we could answer the real question that is in the minds and hearts of the writers: Does the individual personality continue after death? Even an answer in the negative would be better than none. It would be at least solid fact from which future thinking could take a clear-cut orientation. But as yet we have been unable to approach that problem in our research. Perhaps it does lie ahead of us in this exploration. We have no intention of shying away from it if it does, and if there is any way of dealing with it by sound scientific method and provided there is any evidence to lay hold of.

It is true that some men of scientific standing, both in the past and in the present, have come to believe in the personal survival of man beyond death. But this is no proof that immortality has any scientific verification. The scientists who have believed in it have largely done so out of conviction by simple faith, philosophic argument, or the evidence from mediumship. Those of them who have reached their opinion on the basis of work with mediums have not demonstrated their case for science itself, and I feel that they would agree with me in admitting the fact. In part they have been persuaded by personal insights not easily generalizable for others. Whether or not they are right, their case for belief in life after death is not a general scientific one.

What we have so far found in the ESP research would be at least favorable to the *possibility* of survival of personality after death. That is, such survival would naturally entail existence without bodily sense organs, nervous system, and brain. The phenomenon of telepathic perception might afford a theoretical basis for such communion as may be supposed to obtain in such a state. If knowledge of the world about us were possible to a surviving personality, it would be so only through extra-sensory perception of objects, which would be clair-voyance. And so on. Only if minds in general— normal minds—possess these capacities of extra-sensory perception could they possibly exist without the senses and without the sensory organs. To that extent these correspondents may feel that our work has at least a slight bearing on their prob-lems. But possibility is far from probability.

Such letters as these keep us alive to the old but ever vital problem of immortality, which all men at some time face and which is one of the most im-portant and most frequently asked of humanity's questions. But there is much preliminary work to be done, a great deal of exploration into the nature of man's capacities, before we can safely come to grips with this haunting question. And while our strongest feelings urge us to haste, it would be at the sacrifice of all that science has learned through-out its centuries if we were to go ahead too fast, at the expense of safety. Too often before have men sought to answer this question prematurely and inadequately.

10

In many respects the most gratifying letters of all are those from people who want to work with us in one way or another. We have had a sizable number of requests for an opportunity to work in our laboratory—though sometimes the writers put it another way and offer us their services. The spirit behind letters of this sort is encouraging, but we have to reply in the negative most of the time, on the grounds of the correspondent's unfitness for the work. We explain that no one can be invited to conduct research in the laboratory at Duke who has not first independently demonstrated his capacity for it by actual research along parapsychological lines in some other place.

And even for those who qualify on this point it is not always possible for us to accede to the request. Our own schedule of research is heavy, and although our laboratory facilities have been greatly expanded in the last seven years, both in physical space and in fellowship provisions, there are still limitations. The time and energies of the two full-time and four part-time (graduate student) members of the parapsychology staff who work with me are not inexhaustible. We feel, moreover, that if the correspondent is connected with the academic world he can be of greater service by working not at Duke but in his own college or university. The need for independent centers of research is great, and the time has come to divide the work and avoid any danger of overconcentration in one place.

Many of the people who want to experiment with ESP are not academic, and in the early years of our work the majority were either laymen or professional men unconnected with any college. Interest in our work spread next to undergraduate students in other colleges, and ultimately to psychologists on the staffs of universities and colleges in many parts of the country. For this tendency we are most grateful because it multiplies the rate of progress into the field of extra-sensory perception.

When we received letters from laymen, or from doctors (who seem as a class to be unusually interested in what we are doing) or schoolteachers or ministers in which the writers expressed a desire to experiment, we were glad to co-operate even if the correspondents in some cases wrote with a healthy skepticism. Hundreds and hundreds of decks of cards and mimeographed sheets of instructions for testing were sent to such people, even though the increasing extent to which we were supplying these research materials was a drain on our resources. This year, fortunately, the fact that the standard ESP cards (recently improved slightly and of two types, plain and colored) and a standard record pad can be secured in the ordinary bookstores and other places makes it possible for as many laymen to work on ESP problems as have the desire.

Certainly these lay researches have already contributed a great deal to our work, and these letters of inquiry have often led to the setting up of useful research projects. In most cases they are concerned nowadays with the problems of the nature of the ESP process, and spring out of such questions as: "What effect will a certain condition, such as age, or sex, or state of mind have on ESP scores?" "Does ESP improve with practice?" "What is the effect of emotion on the scores?" Work on these and other points has grown to such an extent that on outlet had to be found for the findings. That is why the *Journal of Parapsychology* was founded in the spring of 1937. In fact, a recent survey numbered about fifty such explorations under way since 1934, of which forty have reached some conclusion. Seven have ended in failure to secure anything but chance averages from their tests, but thirty-three have produced results indicating the presence of an extra-chance factor, presumably ESP. This is enough to indicate how important our correspondence has been in helping to further the research, and to indicate that we have had ample reason to appreciate our increased mail, even though sometimes it becomes too voluminous to answer with the care and individual attention it merits.

CHAPTER XV

The Problem of Time

MANY OF THE LETTERS SENT TO US ASK ONE PAR-
ticular kind of question, and perhaps the same problem has already occurred to some of the readers of
this book. It is such an intricate and important matter that it deserves a chapter of its own merely to
suggest what we have been doing about it. In the
broadest general terms, the question is: What is
the relationship, if any, between extra-sensory perception and time?

Our correspondents put the point to us in many
different ways: "Have you tried attempting to predict the order of the cards as they will be after you
shuffle them?" "Have you ever tested prophecy?"
"Do you believe clairvoyance can go into the future?" "Can your subjects call what the order of
cards was in a deck which has been reshuffled?" "Is
the mind able to overcome the barriers of time as it
has those of space?"

These are intelligent and penetrating questions,
and I wish it were possible to answer them in some
other way than the only one so far permissible.
"Yes," we write to the correspondents who raise
this point, "we have tried to solve the general prob-

lem of time and extra-sensory perception, and we
are still trying. We may be working at the same job
for a long time to come; your question is a vitally
significant one and we want to find an answer to
it, no matter what sort of answer it turns out to
be or how long it takes us to arrive at it. We feel
that it is not too much to say that this may be the
greatest question science has ever investigated, and
we are beginning to think it may also prove the
hardest to solve."

Generally I continue my reply by explaining how
our tests on this problem began and describe the
methods we used at the start. So many people have
been interested in this ancient (if not scientifically
honorable) question that it is only fair to explain
here as much as we can safely affirm about it, but
before I do so a warning is necessary. Many things
about our research into this question of time will
have to be left unsaid for the time being. This is
not in order to create any sense of mystery in the
reader's mind, but because we must be sure of our
conclusions before we express them. And there is
nothing about the entire series of problems concerning this time-condition on ESP on which we
are ready to draw definite conclusions.

It would not be fair to the research and to the
great amount of work already performed to say
that no progress at all has been made. Many steps
forward have been taken, much data has been collected, and more than once we thought the goal

was within reach. Each time another, if not a higher, barrier rose up to block our advance. It is essential to emphasize once again that what we were trying to do was to find scientific proof that "prophecy" in the sense of knowledge of future events or *precognition* was either a fact or *not* a fact. We were aware, of course, that it was also important to establish the truth or falsity of *retrocognition*, clairvoyance into the past.

The story of our four years of ups and downs, our long running struggle with the complexities of this research, must wait until we know how it comes out, but I should like to explain its relationship to the work presented in this book and to our whole research, and tell a little of how we came to undertake it.

2

A good deal was said in the earlier part of this book about the debt which the scientific investigation of ESP owes to the anecdotes of psychic experience, and the possibility of precognition or previsionary ESP is naturally associated with many of those stories. Surveying them carefully, as we did, for clues to the nature of the phenomenon we were investigating, it was impossible to overlook that element of futurity. A large portion of the inexplicable personal experiences appeared to involve a foresight of the future apparently not to be explained away by reason, and many people have been led to believe that such extra-rational prediction of events is possible for some persons under some conditions.

In most respects the stories describing experiences in which some kind of prophecy or prevision appeared to be manifest were similar to other psychic anecdotes. I scarcely need to give again examples of these familiar incidents, but the typical story runs something like this: A mother has a vivid and alarming impression of a train wreck. She may be asleep and see the wreck in a nightmare, or she may have a waking hallucination, or an intuitive experience. The impression of the wreck is more or less definitely associated in her mind with her son (or her daughter), and perhaps also with some definite place, such as a tunnel. The dream or hallucination is so powerful that she feels it has a special meaning for her. It turns out later that her son was actually injured in a wreck at the spot where her dream assigned it. There are many stories of this description, and in almost half the cases, roughly, the dream or impression actually precedes the substantiating occurrence. In other cases the dream and the event occur simultaneously, or nearly so.

If one cares to give any credence to these experiences, they suggest that time is not an important factor in them. Where unusual knowledge is somehow genuinely conveyed it is almost as likely to be knowledge of the future as of the present or the past. To many students of psychology or of science

in general this very fact might appear sufficient to
warrant dismissing the whole range of such anecdotes as absurd and impossible. Yet as I suggested
in Chapter II there can be no harm in investigating whether something lies behind stories of unexplainable occurrences, provided we proceed in
our examination by careful experiment and with
scientific impartiality.

People who are familiar with the numerous collections of supposedly precognitive experiences will
not be inclined to dismiss the subject lightly, though
they may wisely reserve decision and belief on the
question. There is one particular collection of
precognitive experiences that has awakened wide interest in recent years—J. W. Dunne's *An Experiment With Time*. The anecdotal part of the book
mainly consists of the author's own dream experiences which have turned out, he reports, to be more
or less previsionary. Dunne goes on to say that he
persuaded other people to keep a record of their
dreams, and that when they did so they found many
instances of extra-rational foreknowledge of the
next day's events. Theodore Besterman of the English Society for Psychical Research attempted to repeat the observations of this semiexperimental
phase of Dunne's case but without appreciable success. Dunne did not think the conditions of Besterman's work were entirely the same as those of his
own.

His book presents an interesting and ingenious

theory to explain precognition, but there is no reason for our going into it unless and until we find that prophecy and prophetic dreams are actually true. Meanwhile, it is clear that some of Dunne's own experiences can easily be explained by simple extra-sensory perception. He apparently was unwilling to accept the possibility of ESP but found it easier to believe in precognition, and illogical as that may appear, his anecdotes and the discussions of them are thought-provoking. They do not, however, make out the proved, experimental case which science must demand on so momentous a question.

I am often asked why we at Duke have not followed up Dunne's method of keeping a record of as many dreams as possible and checking on their accuracy. The reason is that the estimation of success or failure is so difficult. It is hard to judge the hits and the misses in a description of a dream, or to tell how good a hit is when there is one. In working with such vague, unclassifiable material as dreams, and attempting to check them against the multitudinous events of a day, week, or even year, there is no way of applying a sound measure of evaluation. Dunne's method demands reliance upon someone's general judgment on points of correctness and value, and this is too uncertain a criterion even for questions less important than this one. Either precognition must be tested by a clear-cut experimental procedure, with unambiguous logic, or it must remain a relatively unsolved problem.

More impressive than Dunne's work, at least to me, are such collections as those of Mr. H. F. Saltmarsh, published by the English Society for Psychical Research, and *L'Avenir et la Prémonition* by the late Professor Charles Richet, a widely respected physiologist. Saltmarsh's clarification and analysis, in particular, compel a certain respect for his evidence. The cases he cites were carefully selected from a larger number and come only from reputable witnesses and reporters. Each is backed by corroboratory reports. In these cases Saltmarsh found a degree of internal consistency which he tried to evaluate, and he was himself convinced that precognition was the only adequate explanation.

Only by doubting the authenticity of the cases which Saltmarsh has compiled can the reader question his conclusion. But when I recall the high mortality of truth in general testimony, when 65 per cent is a liberal figure to assign to the accuracy of the average witness, I am compelled to hold out to the bitter end against any such method of establishing precognition. There must be an experimental test of the question, and as rigorous a one as we can possibly devise.

3

Dunne, Richet, and Saltmarsh have raised the question of prophecy, but its solution still awaits experimental verification. The evidence based on psychic anecdotes suggests that time is no limitation to spontaneous experiences of various sorts. How does this suggestion coincide with the results of our work at Duke and with the accepted theories of space, matter, and energy?

The distance tests gave evidence that space is not a limiting condition on the ESP ability. When we stop to think that time and space go inseparably together in every known, measurable event in nature, that we even speak in science of our "space-time continuum," it looks as if ESP should be as free of limitation by time as it is by space. To be *in* a spatial system is to be in a temporal system as well. To be *out* of a spatial system, it appears logical to suppose, would entail being out of a temporal system. And if, indeed, mind can escape from temporal limits it would, of course, be able to go forward to future events or back to past ones.

The very conception of "getting out of time" and still continuing to exist gets quickly beyond an easy understanding or explanation. So, also, does precognition of an "as yet unhappened" event, however logical the argument from the conquest of space by ESP makes its appear. True, many concepts of modern physics rest solely on logical considerations of this general sort, but while I find the logic unassailable, and while it leads to the same conclusion as do the anecdotes, neither stories nor logic are as valid to me as experiments, and I shall adhere to my determination not to accept or reject precognition until actual tests have rendered the verdict, if, indeed, they ever do.

When we began our experiments on precognition, or previsionary clairvoyance, I thought the experimentation would be simple. We had what seemed to be a good working technique—based on the use of the cards. All we had to do was to ask a subject to call the cards as they would be at some point in the future. It seemed to us that after the most exhaustive research we should be able to devise, either the scores of our subjects' tests would exhibit significance, in which case ESP would demonstrably have conquered time, or they would not, in which case we should have arrived at a valuable and important negative conclusion. So we wasted no time in turning some of our highest scoring subjects to this new venture in exploration. They were asked to call the order of the cards as they would be after shuffling. Then the deck was shuffled according to specifications, either a given number of times, or in a mechanical shuffler, or for a fixed length of time. The actual order of the deck, after the shuffling was over, was checked against the calls the subject had made beforehand.

This approach to the problem of the penetrability of the future was a simple one and grew naturally out of the research in extra-sensory perception already described in this book. It dealt with just one more of a long series of conditions under which ESP had been tested. It seemed likely that there would be no more difficulty in this project than in a test of any other of a dozen methods and variations made through the seven years of active pursuit of ESP problems.

Obviously, had the attempt so hopefully begun nearly four years ago been either a flat failure or a brilliant success there would be no occasion for the restraint I am now exercising in this discussion. But the deceptive simplicity of the job at the start gave place in time to an almost bewildering complexity of problems that we are only now finding a way to overcome.

Can we ever control these time experiments sufficiently to prove anything? Nobody before us had excluded clairvoyance from telepathy tests. We thought we did that, but we have not adequately excluded possible precognition from all our tests for clairvoyance. The results *could be* due to precognitive telepathy. The subject might be looking ahead to the checkup. Our telepathy tests *could be* due to precognitive clairvoyance. So it goes. What have we? How far shall we look ahead, suppose these mere logical possibilities, and handle our tests so as to anticipate all conceivable future criticisms, no matter how absurd they seem to us now? If we do conjure up all the mere possibilities, will we ever get anywhere? On the other hand, how can we come out with a claim to have proved the occurrence of precognition, and leave untested logical though unsubstantiated alternatives to endanger our conclusions? This is the dilemma we have before us.

All our precognition thus far is based on card work. We call the cards as they will be, predicting an order. These calls are recorded. Then investigators cut or shuffle the pack, and finally check the cards against the calls. If we attempt to avoid precognitive telepathy by having the subject shuffle and cut the cards himself, and even do the actual checking, we are still not out of the woods. If by unconscious clairvoyance a subject can cut a pack so as to favor the recorded calls or, in shuffling, can place the cards by clairvoyant knowledge in a better position in the pack, then he would score above chance average. In this way, after making a prophecy he might, even unintentionally, fix the cards clairvoyantly so as to make it come true. The idea may seem silly at first, but it is a most serious disturbance to the research. Down goes our precognition "house of cards" in what we might call a "psychic shuffle." What use to say that it seems incredible to get a subject to know the whole pack by clairvoyance when one card at a time seems hard enough? Practically incredible, yes, but logically possible on the strength of our own work! The question is, how far shall we go in taking these

logical possibilities seriously? Will we ever get anywhere if we do, and can we ever be sure if we don't?

4

The same difficulties which apply to the research
on precognition have arisen in our work on the companion problem of retrocognition, or extra-sensory
perception of things in the past. Not as much has
been said about this question so far, and probably
it is not as generally exciting and spectacular as the
idea of penetrating the future. Yet it is clearly
a necessary part of the experimentation on the relation of ESP to time.

Exactly the same series of logical arguments that
led us to predict that we should find evidence of
precognition in our card tests applied with equal
force to the probability of extra-sensory perception
of the unrecorded past. We believed, too, that if
we did find evidence that time was no barrier to
ESP, many people would be more willing to accept
a demonstration based on retrocognition and find
it easier, on the whole, to understand.

Curiously enough, it is harder to investigate
retrocognition than precognition. Really crucial
tests, ones which will eliminate all possibility, for
example, of the subject's actually perceiving the
record against which his calls will ultimately be
checked instead of the past order of the cards, are
difficult to devise. There are some of us, in fact, who

fear that the hypothesis of retrocognition may prove truly untestable, but it would be scientifically rash to say so definitely at the present stage of our work.

5

The great trouble in working with problems of the mind is that it is hard to draw sharp lines and keep each thing we want to work with in its own separate test tube, as it were. For example, it took a long time in the history of ESP research before telepathy and clairvoyance were experimentally separated. Now, suppose someone asks, as one of my friends did, how we know that the subject in ordinary clairvoyance tests does not actually use precognitive telepathy, "previsioning" from the mind of the experimenter the order of the symbols when the latter ultimately looks at them in recording and checking the results. My friend (like Mr. Dunne) finds it easier to suppose both precognition and telepathy than clairvoyance and she can find some other way of interpreting almost all our evidence on clairvoyance, in line with her favorite theory. Almost, but not quite, all of it. It requires a very special experiment indeed to escape her objection, and though it has been performed, it has not yet been published in scientific form, and I shall therefore not go into it here.

I mention this problem merely to illustrate on a simpler case what type of trouble we have in greater measure when we tackle precognition. One elusive alternative interpretation after another turns up as at least a logical possibility. As in the case just mentioned, we do not need to believe the other interpretation to be the true one, or even very reasonable; if it is barely possible we must as scientists recognize it and disprove or prove its validity.

The place of the mind in time—or the place of time in the mind, to put it another way—cannot yet be represented as demonstrated by any procedure which we and other research workers have been able to devise *beyond all possibility of an alternative explanation*. In other words, we are not ready to draw conclusions as to whether ESP is limited by time or not.

The universe has been guarding some of its secrets from man's understanding for thousands and thousands of years. We believed at the start that our approach to the problem of prevision was a good one, and in spite of four years of alternate frustration and promise we are still far from discouraged. It may, of course, happen that the intense critical analysis which we have tried to give our work at every step thus far will find fatal flaws in experiments which even at this moment suggest a final solution. To feel convinced either way beforehand is to violate the spirit of science.

CHAPTER XVI

From Now On

THIS CHAPTER IS A FINAL ONE ONLY IN THE SENSE that it is the last one in the book. It is not a stopping place. The research about which I have been writing has not halted; we continue to test for possible subjects, find new ones able to score well, and capable workers go on being drawn into the investigation. In most cases they are finding in their own work the same order of success reported in these pages. But this story of the work at Duke has now covered everything that has been tested according to academic custom by presentation in scientific publications, and here is, therefore, a logical place to pause.

It should not, however, be regarded as a place to present conclusions. Those should be reached only at the safest possible time—after they are no longer needed. When conclusions are forced upon us by the results of experiments designed to bring them or their contraries to crucial issue we can begin to speak of them with assurance and safety. And though we have been carrying on our investigation for a long time, and in spite of our continuing enthusiasm based on the progress we have made so far, there are few and not very secure conclusions to be drawn.

Instead, looking back across the intervening chapters to the one which opened this book, to the initial statement of the goal, it is best to realign ourselves with its intent. In that light we can estimate our present position and consider the course for the future.

2

The general purpose of our research was described in Chapter I. It was to find out, if we could, something that would enable us to place the mind of man in a definite relation to the world of law and causation which our senses and our sciences have represented to us.

"What is the human mind?" we asked, as men have been asking for centuries. We posed the question as still the most fundamental in modern psychology if not in life itself. It seemed possible to find a new approach to this question by re-examining and investigating an ancient and accepted doctrine of our science—the belief that *nothing* can enter the mind except through the gateways of the recognized senses. This psychological dogma had become, we pointed out, an old and almost undisputed frontier of the mind, one that has had much to do with shaping the general views of its nature which we hold today.

The research itself represents a critical testing

of this dogma of the inviolability of the mind's sensory frontier. If we could find any extra-sensory avenue to knowledge, not only would that concept cease to be the circumscribing law of mind it was once considered, but a new frontier, a further horizon would be established.

That new frontier has now been established unless all of us who have been exploring it by years of testing and many hundreds of thousands of trials have been completely and continuingly self-deluded or incompetent, not only at the Duke laboratory but elsewhere as well. Either delusion is the explanation of our results or else we have found proof that the mind of man does indeed have an extra-sensory way of perceiving, and hence, whether we like it or not, the old frontier must go the way of Newtonian mechanics in the light of relativity.

The case is as strong as the evidence, and no stronger. The reader must judge that strength against his own background and criteria of evidence. If the canons of scientific judgment by which he reaches a decision are too high for the experimental data to prove conclusive for him, then he must wait in suspended judgment for an ultimate answer to the questions we set out to investigate. He will hardly be able to decide that ESP does *not* occur since there has never been and could not well be any downright proof that perception beyond the senses does not occur. Even if all the trials we made to find proof of ESP had been failures, one

might protest that perhaps the conditions for finding it were not right. And this would be more than
sheer technical haggling in the case of any mental
phenomenon of an extremely weak and delicate
character. But when the large majority of the tests
performed to repeat our original ESP work confirm
our findings and demonstrate that the senses are not
the only channels of cognition this supposition need
not be considered. To me it seems most unlikely that
anyone with a thorough knowledge of what we have
done in the research will be able to reject its results
completely.

3

What recognition of ESP may mean when it is
fully realized is not possible to say or desirable to
conjecture. Everyone will realize without long reflection that its bearing is not upon psychology
alone, or even science as a whole. It can scarcely
fail to have an immense influence on the life of both
individuals and groups. But what influence? What
bearings? Who at this point would "rush in" to say?
We need only read the premature judgments that
accompanied earlier scientific discoveries and inven-
tions to seal our lips against the impulse to predict.

Still, there is nothing to prevent the reader himself from reflecting over the question of ESP and
its possible meaning for his own life, his profession,
his social world. I see nothing wrong with his sup-
posing that as research continues we *may* find out

how to control the process and turn it to proper
uses, to educational and social advantage, to personal, economic, and scientific enterprise—to almost whatever you will. But these speculations must
be the reader's own. I do not say they never occur
in my own thinking. But my belief is that this kind
of speculation can wait, and had better wait for the
research to catch up with it.

We who are going ahead with the investigation
require no greater stimulus than the work itself
provides. No specific application is necessary to encourage our efforts, and more enthusiasm for the
work could hardly help it, since all of us already find
it an exciting and rewarding enterprise. There is
even sometimes danger in our anticipating its implications too far in advance of the test results, because some of these bearings quickly evoke our own
strongest interests and deepest yearnings. And
finally the world at large may all too quickly con-
vert half-proved truth into the whole belief it naturally wants.

In these final paragraphs, then, though I realize
that many of the people who read this book may be
looking for some word as to what *we* think the
research may lead to, and are expecting the last
chapter to enlarge upon what progress has been
made, I am practicing with regret the advice I so
often have dealt out to others by way of the mailbag: in a word, to stick to the tests and let applications and interpretations wait. They will be all the

better when we are forced to them by the very weight of the evidence.

Above all, I would be reluctant to aid and abet the many extra-academic cults and schools of thought and belief by any unwise remark as to the meaning of these experiments. I realize with some misgivings that the research is already looming large in the teachings of these groups. The well-established facts are theirs and welcome. I shrink only when I consider that the things which may be made the most of by some of these orders and societies may be just what is least established or only mentioned as a hypothesis.

It might be expected from the history of psychology (which is so largely the rise and fall of academic schools of thought) that the growth of ESP research and discussion will at length evolve a new school or branch of psychological thought. I should regard this as an incomparably pernicious outcome. There is, I believe, more than a mere play of words in the opinion that psychology will never become a mature science until its school days are over. The successful avoidance of this outcome for ESP lies only in keeping clear of hasty interpretation and sticking close to the facts.

4

To the explorer who is moving forward through these problems the situation is a happy one and the outlook for the future highly alluring. He is less concerned with what has already been done than he is with the completion of the full scientific exploration of ESP. What is this newly found process? To say it is *not* sensory is not to say what it *is*, and not even to establish a clearly defined negative, because *sensory* experience itself, familiar though it is, still represents a great gap in our understanding.

A phenomenon is understood, in science and anywhere else, by its relations within itself and to the rest of the body of knowledge, and the first great job ahead is that of finding out all about ESP, discovering all possible relations it holds to other mental, bodily, and external processes. By discovering what ESP links up with, what helps it, what interferes with it, and where and how to find it and control it, we hope eventually to win sufficient mastery of this unusual power of mind to bring it wholly within the scope of science. Then, I believe, is the time to consider applications—when they are demonstrable, and when the natural disposition of skeptics to ridicule can have no provocation.

Deeply as I am involved in the earnest search for the nature of ESP, for the secret of its control, for the place it fits into the mind—its scope, its power, and its development—my devotion to this is divided. Still more attractive to me, I confess, perhaps against my better judgment, is what may lie beyond ESP. Perhaps it is the frontiersman's disposition conceivably resident in many of us that makes the appeal of the problems that lie over the next barrier so great.

Immediately beyond ESP lie the great living problems of time, precognition, and retrocognition. Can mind free itself from time in ESP as it does from space? Logically, as we saw in the preceding chapter, it should be expected to do so. But if precognition should occur, it would raise more questions of the profoundest sort about the nature of the universe than I should care to contemplate. Again, then, let us say with that great contributor to both science and its methods, Sir Isaac Newton, "Let hypotheses alone until the facts require them." I, for one, cannot let these great challenging problems alone, but I reaffirm here my belief in sharp restraint of speculation beyond the range of experimental test.

Even a prudent and restrained logical glimpse beyond ESP itself reveals one great problem beyond another, like giant peaks that silently challenge ascent. I should not want to name these master problems that lie so far beyond, for they may not be realities. No matter. The lure is there. If from these future adventures we attain an evidential eminence from which still further frontiers of the mind of man are visible, who would prefer to have stood with Balboa on a peak in Darien for that initial sight of a new ocean or even on the bow of the *Santa Maria* for the first happy glimpse of the outlines of a new world!

THE END

ESP TEST CARDS AND SCORE PAD

TWO DIFFERENT PACKS OF ESP TEST CARDS ARE NOW PUBLICLY AVAILABLE, AS WELL AS A SCORE PAD ON WHICH TO NOTE DOWN CARD CALLS AND SCORES.

EACH PACK CONSISTS OF 25 CARDS, 5 EACH OF THE 5 SYMBOLS PICTURED.

PACK I (PLAIN ESP TEST CARDS) IS SUITABLE FOR MOST TESTS. THE SYMBOLS OF ALL 5 "SUITS" ARE PRINTED IN BLACK ON A WHITE BACKGROUND.

PACK II (COLOR ESP TEST CARDS) IS SUITABLE FOR ALL TESTS. THE BACKGROUND OF THE CARDS IN THIS PACK, WHICH IS NOT ILLUSTRATED HERE, IS BLACK, AND EACH SYMBOL IS PRINTED IN A DIFFERENT COLOR: THE PLUS IN RED, THE WAVES IN BLUE, THE STAR IN GREEN, THE CIRCLE IN YELLOW, AND THE SQUARE IN WHITE.

ADDITIONAL READING

The reader who may be interested in examining further material on ESP is referred to the following books and periodicals:

Extra-Sensory Perception, by J. B. Rhine (Foreword by Professor William McDougall; Introduction by Dr. W. F. Prince). 169 pp. Illustrated. Boston: Bruce Humphries, 1935.

Handbook for ESP Tests, A, arranged and edited by C. E. Stuart and J. G. Pratt (Preface by J. B. Rhine). Illustrated. New York: Farrar & Rinehart, Inc., 1937.

Journal of Parapsychology, The (quarterly), Duke University Press, Durham, N. C. (Published on the first days of March, June, September, December.) Illustrated.

Earlier reports of various investigations into extra-sensory phenomena will be found in the *Proceedings* of the English Society for Psychical Research (London), and in Bulletin XVI of the Boston Society for Psychic Research.

Two popular accounts of interest are:

Mental Radio, by Upton Sinclair (Introduction by Professor William McDougall). 239 pp. Illustrated. Pasadena, Calif.: Upton Sinclair, 1930.

Telepathy and Clairvoyance, by Rudolf Tischner (Translation by W. D. Hutchinson; Introduction by E. J. Dingwall). 226 pp. New York: Harcourt, Brace & Co., Inc., 1925.